The Square Root of Someone

By

Anne Brandt

ISBN: 0-75963-134-4

This book is printed on acid free paper.

1stBooks - rev. 8/24/01

"Tattoo" originally appeared in *Seniors*. "Meeting My Father" and "Gracia's Piano" originally appeared in *The Chicago Tribune Magazine*. "1925 Holly" originally appeared in *The Denver Post* as "The House on Holly Street."

To Judi, Joan, and Kyle—Without your help,
this book might still be in a drawer.

Contents

Grand Tour

In the 1930s, my Grandfather Jim studied to be a doctor in Vienna, Austria, while my Grandmother Anna stayed behind with three young children in upstate New York. When he returned home, he promised her that the two of them would visit Europe together someday.

But other things came first. There was a career to establish and children to raise and patients who needed him. Three decades later, there was the cancer that claimed him.

But Grandmother still wanted to see Europe, so she decided her oldest grandchild would accompany her. I was fourteen.

In words not spoken but just as binding, I was to be a traveling companion, a surrogate husband, for my Grandmother. We would replicate the trip that had been in the back of my grandparents' minds for most of their marriage.

My mother was thrilled that I would take this trip. She was a single parent, and her relief at having me occupied for another summer vacation was clearly visible. She and Grandmother spent hours making arrangements and checking things off their to-do lists. They got passports and visas and appointments for physicals. They scheduled our departure from New York City and determined when we had to be there to board the Queen Mary, the ship that would take us across the Atlantic. For once in their lives, these two women were in agreement.

In all the planning, no one asked what I thought. If they had, they would have heard that going to Europe was at the bottom on my list of things to do. At fourteen, this was my last free summer. I was old enough to enjoy its pleasures but not so old as to be burdened by a part-time job or summer school for extra credit. I was also madly in love.

While Mother and Grandmother made their plans, the object of my affection and I talked about lazy days at the local swimming pool or at the ice cream counter of Elsworth's Drugstore. We talked about walking up to Forest Park on Wednesday nights to watch the local parish boys' baseball team. We talked about catching movie matinees, instead of having to pay the evening rate.

We both knew what my mother and hers were planning, but we pretended it wouldn't happen. We couldn't believe it. We held hands and said silent prayers. But on the appointed date, which just happened to be the day after my birthday, I relinquished dreams of lazy days at the swimming pool and went to New York City. We sailed for France on the Queen Mary two days later.

Grandmother and I became a couple at the dinner hour on board ship and in hotel registers across the continent. We spent seven weeks visiting nine countries and uncountable churches. I saw da Vinci's Mona Lisa in France and Michelangelo's Sistine Chapel in Italy. From the tinted windows of a tour bus, Anne Frank's hideaway, bombed out ruins, and newly constructed superhighways sped by.

I tried to be dutiful. When Grandmother wanted the light off at nine o'clock, we flipped the switch. If she wanted to have breakfast at seven, we rose in time to brush our teeth and dress. When she wanted grapefruit before her oatmeal, I ordered the same, all the while wishing I were back in St. Louis watching the parish boys lose their baseball game.

Once in Salerno, Italy, I went on an afternoon walk alone. Perhaps I was gone an hour, more likely two. But no one knew where I was, and when I returned Grandmother was beside herself with panic that some Italian had whisked me away forever. In the privacy of our bathroom, she let me know I had caused her grave concern and it was not to happen again. She threatened to send me home if it did; and, while I toyed with the idea to gain my freedom, the shame that would have accompanied it held me in check until we returned to the United States deep in August.

My high school friends were glad to see me but disinterested in my travels. Europe was something they read about in history texts, since their grandmothers could never have afforded such a trip for one person, much less two. On the other hand, my mother wanted to hear everything. My role as surrogate traveler was not yet finished.

My boyfriend had spent the summer sharpening his pitching skills and listening to baseball on the radio. I had listened to tour guides describe the rise and fall of Western civilization. By September, each of us spoke a different language, and we never recaptured the innocent fun of those early summer plans.

Neither Grandmother nor I ever mentioned the Grand Tour of Europe to the other again. Yet, forty years later, I still keep a box of souvenirs that includes a menu from the Captain's dinner aboard ship, a keyring from Salerno, and a photograph of my grandmother and me in front of the Coliseum in Rome. Looking in her eyes now, I see a sadness that runs counterpoint to her smile; and I realize that she must have missed her husband on that long-ago trip as much as I missed the boy of my youth.

Montmarte

She was in her late sixties, and years of travel to Everywhere were stamped on her passport. But wherever she went, she had one idiosyncrasy.

My mother never stayed in fancy hotels. Why pay for a posh room, her argument went, when she would only use it for sleeping. Instead, she found lodging in fringe areas that never saw four stars.

And that is how we ended up in a petite hotel in Montmarte the last time we visited Paris together. I don't think she even noticed the obvious comparison to the "red light" district of any major American city. Nor did it bother her that the bathroom was a long walk down the hall.

Our second floor room looked out on the front of the hotel. In turn, the hotel fronted a square that boasted a carousel and a café. Across the square was a Catholic church with a banner stretching between its farthest corners that begged tourists to make a contribution to its renovation. Mother would have approved of the effort to preserve the church, but would never have donated a dime.

After checking in and dumping our bags, we left the hotel in search of an early dinner. There were many small restaurants to choose from in the neighborhood, and she found a little French bistro to her liking only a few blocks away. That night, over a bottle of red wine, Mother let down her perpetual guard and reminisced about her childhood and mine. She talked of her parents and of leaving home. She talked of marrying my father and then divorcing him when I was still a child.

Mother loved to travel. She often told about her first trip, at age nineteen, when she had saved enough money to fly from New York City to Syracuse in the morning and back on the same afternoon. From that day forward, she decided that she would be an airline stewardess. And when my mother decided something, it was as good as done. She applied to Trans World Airlines and became a stewardess long before men sought the position and the title became that of flight attendant.

Mother loved the job; but it was during World War II and, like many young women, she met a soldier after she'd been on the airlines a while. He proposed. She accepted.

In those days, married women were not allowed to work on the airlines, so Mother resigned. My mother and father married on Valentine's Day, and I arrived two years later. Although the marriage didn't last, her love of travel did.

The first trip I remember taking with my mother occurred the summer I turned ten. We crossed the United States, from New York to Oregon and back, by train. That was in the day when railroads were considered a fine method of transportation, instead of simply a way to carry freight from Point A to Point B. Mother, who always maintained an open door policy in her own home, had friends all along the way who owed her free lodging; so we rode the train from one home to the next, spending a few days here and a few days there. We didn't stay in a single hotel.

When I was in high school, Mother announced at the beginning of one summer that she wanted to save four hundred dollars and treat us to a trip to New Orleans for Thanksgiving. Both four hundred dollars and New Orleans seemed like unimaginable extravagances to me, but I agreed to do my share by giving up our weekly dinner at the local cafeteria. I really did not see how this would make a difference; but if Mother said it would, then it was so.

Sure enough, at the beginning of November she bought two coach railway tickets and took me out of school a day early during Thanksgiving Week so that we could be in New Orleans for the traditional turkey dinner. Since we knew no one in the city, Mother broke down and made reservations for the smallest room at the Monteleone Hotel in the center of the French Quarter.

"Do you remember," she'd say to me in later years, "The Thanksgiving dinner in New Orleans?"

I wasn't obliged to answer, but I always nodded.

"Remember how they turned off the lights at dessert time and asked everyone in the restaurant to light a match? It was like a thousand twinkling stars."

As a rule Mother kept these memories—and many others—to herself. But this particular night in the French bistro in Montmarte, with the Paris lights twinkling like the thousand matches of long ago, she was as warm and charming and gentle as I ever remember; and we shared secrets back and forth, made more special by a second bottle of Cabernet. Silly and tired, we strolled back to the hotel.

As always, Mother fell asleep immediately. But before she shut her eyes for the night, I remember her rising up on one arm from the bed and saying in miserable French, "Shut the door, Anne, shut the door."

I smiled in the dark. This remarkable woman could master the Metro but her tongue could not conquer the French language. "Shut the door" was her American way of saying "I love you" in French.

"Je t'adore, Mamma, je t'adore," I whispered back, hoping she had heard me.

Gray Cloud Syndrome

Gray clouds make a sure thing tentative.

The family planning a picnic at the beach waits to see if rain materializes. The tourist hoping to snap the best outdoor shot hurries with his camera. The housewife grabs armfuls of sheets off the laundry line, just in case.

And when gray clouds take up residence in the landscape of the mind, the result is the same. Things won't work out, not today.

Gray cloud syndrome has visited me often over the years, although the intervals between its appearance are becoming further and further apart.

In the beginning, the clouds latched onto me with a tenacity I neither understood nor resisted. Perhaps if I'd understood them better, my resistance would have been greater. But all I knew back then was that some shift occurred in my life that let the clouds in and the gloom take over.

Usually, it wasn't even a large shift, like flunking an important exam or worrying about a boyfriend. It was more often much smaller, more subtle. Had this shift occurred on a day when the sun shone in my soul, it would have been ignored.

Once I learned three college girlfriends went to dinner without me. These were my closest chums, long time confidantes. Why would they do this? What had I done to be excluded?

And that's how it starts. The clouds gather, moving with the same swiftness with which I mentally moved from dinner to breaking off our friendship. The clouds whisper, "You're no longer one of them. You're all alone."

For two or three days, I made lame excuses when the same friends wanted to meet in the Student Union or go to Hamilton's after class for a beer. I didn't sit with them or participate in discussions during Sociology 243 or Theology 310. Instead, I hid in the second floor women's lounge and slept.

Of course, this was over-reaction at its best, but that's the insidious quality of mental gray clouds.

I learned the truth later. My friends had telephoned with an invitation to join their dinner party; but this was before the days of call waiting, answering machines, and cell phones. When they didn't reach anyone at my home, they figured I was out having a good time.

Other, more serious, bouts with clouds occurred during my early marriage, after my children were born, and when their father and I divorced. Each time, the clouds clung and immobilized me, until I finally sought professional help.

"Do you think I'm depressed?" I asked the therapist after several visits. My eyes were red, and my hands held the remnants of tissues and mascara. I'd lost 20 pounds and wore the look of a refugee. In a sense, that's exactly what I was, a refugee far from the familiar homeland of equilibrium.

She nodded her head. The tears came, only this time they were a relief.

"What can I do?"

"I think you've had these experiences many times in your life," she said. "You didn't know they were signs of depression. Because you lived with them, you thought they were normal behavior. But they don't have to be."

We talked at length about depression and its signals; and I left her office with a prescription for an anti-depressant. She warned me it would take about two weeks to have the desired effect, but I should keep taking the medicine regardless of how I felt. Even if the clouds clung tenaciously.

They held firm as I took the little pills twice a day. I could hardly rouse myself from bed each morning to care for my sons, much less get through the day. I was about to be divorced, the mother of two, and truly alone. Life was definitely not worth the effort.

Yet, somehow I struggled through those first two weeks, wondering what to do and how to do it. I spent mornings getting dressed. I spent afternoons at a friend's house working myself up from the well of despair while my children and hers played in the back yard. I spent evenings waiting for my sons to go to bed, so I might follow them and be relieved of thinking, yet knowing the same challenge would present itself again at dawn.

Two weeks to the day I took the first pill the reclamation of sunny skies slowly began. It was a Monday, and my soon-to-be-ex-husband had gone to work early, probably eager to be away from his unhappy wife who was still in bed. The week stretched in front of me, and I was alone with my children.

But instead of burrowing further under the blankets, I awoke and thought of bathing. The clouds still hovered, as I rose before seven and headed for the shower. It was the first time in months that I was dressed and waiting for my sons to make their sleepy appearance in the kitchen. Together the three of us dined on Cheerios®, as I felt a shift in the corners of my mind. It was as if something had shaken loose.

I won't say the day was free of problems, but at nightfall I kissed each boy lovingly and put him to bed. Then I settled into the couch with a book and read a full chapter before succumbing to weariness. But it was a good weariness, one founded in the knowledge that my clouds were less gray and possibly less tenacious.

The next few days became a week and then two. Not every day was better than the one before it; but, over time, the good ones began to outweigh the bad. I took the little pills for almost a year and continued to see the therapist. Both helped change my life.

Today gray cloud syndrome still appears on my horizon, but now I know in my heart that it is as temporary as summer rain.

Patches

Patches didn't take sides. She didn't choose favorites. She had no hidden agenda, unless you consider walking between your legs when you stood by the kitchen door an attempt to sneak outside.

Our cat looked exactly like her name, with various brown markings spread this way and that over her predominantly white body. Despite the common name, however, Patches was elegant and knew it.

My older son, Kevin, found her in an animal shelter needing a home but refusing to beg. He had studied several cats, holding them and evaluating if they were the right one, before coming to the calico's cage. At first she showed no interest, but he persisted until she was wrapped in his ten-year-old arms looking for all the world as if she had chosen him, instead of the other way around.

Ours was a blended family, the kind where the husband and wife both have offspring from other unions and on any given day these offspring may or may not take kindly to each other. Patches didn't care. She took kindly to us all. Every day.

In a blended family, there is little time to adapt to each member's arrival on the scene. My household went from three to six in the time it took to say, "I do." These two little words meant instant and ongoing adjustments. Like accommodating food choices or bedtime routines or favorite television programs. Like making sure you don't treat your husband's children differently from your own while at the same time hoping yours don't notice that there is only half the time for them that you once had.

Patches helped by providing extra attention to whoever needed it. She often moved from child's room to child's room, lounging on the bed, resting in a lap, providing a supporting meow or two.

It is true that she had an advantage.

There may have been other owners in her past, but none had current claim to her. She had no noncustodial parents with visitation rights. Or extra sets of grandparents who wanted to be involved. So she gave her heart more completely than the rest of us. While the human relationships ebbed and flowed, she remained calm and steady.

For example, whenever my stepdaughters returned from a weekend with their mother, it took me a while to feel as if they were really home so I kept my distance for an hour or so. I knew I was doing it and couldn't help myself. But Patches rubbed against their legs as soon as they burst in the kitchen door, as if to say, "I'm glad you're here. I missed you."

She was there through the grade school years and the first-date years and when the oldest child left the nest. She watched four children reach toward adulthood while their parents, custodial and noncustodial alike, moved into early middle age. If Patches aged in the process, nobody noticed.

Until that Friday night.

Keith, my second son, came home from high school at his regular time, but Patches didn't run to the kitchen at the sound of his key in the lock. Rachel, my older stepdaughter, left for her job at the mall. No Patches said goodbye. Finally Stephanie, the youngest, discovered the cat stretched on her bed, hardly breathing; and her cries brought the rest of us from various hiding places. My husband and Keith and I jammed into Steph's room. The cat's eyes were open but held no recognition.

"What shall we do?" Keith asked anyone with an answer.

"The vet," my husband replied.

The rumble of a muffler grew and then died nearby. I heard it and raced downstairs and out the kitchen door, as Kevin braked his car in the driveway. It was the first time all fall he'd come home from the university. He shoved open

11

the driver's door and pulled himself out with a sigh from being wedged behind the steering wheel for three hours.

"Kevin, it's Patches. Something's terribly wrong. We're going to the vet."

"Now?"

I nodded. His exhaustion energized into motion. He bounded past me and into the house to meet my husband coming toward the door, the cat cradled gently in his arms. Kevin went to him and transferred Patches to his own arms.

"My car's in the driveway," he said to my husband. "You drive. I'll hold her."

They headed for the doctor. I raced to the mall and got Rachel excused from work. Within twenty minutes the six of us were gathered in a tiny room where Patches lay on the vet's cold examining table, her eyes closed forever, the invisible glue of our family gone.

We stared at her, beautiful even in death, and talked about what to do. For once we were all in agreement. We would leave the vet with our cat and take her home to be buried in the back yard behind the garage. She had always wanted to be outside; at least now we could honor that wish. Kevin picked her up for the last time, and all I could think of was that first day when he and she found each other. The rest of us followed him out the door.

At home, Kevin dug a deep hole in the ground, and we assembled around it while he laid her down. The night was completely black and clear. My husband wanted to follow his religious tradition, so each of us threw a shovel of dirt over Patches' grave while he gave a touching eulogy. Then we held hands and stood in a circle. There was nothing else to do.

In the days that followed, the girls made a wooden cross from two sticks held perpendicular to each other with purple yarn. Six flat stones appeared over the grave, although no one admitted to putting them there. Photos of Patches taken over the years appeared on the refrigerator, held in place by magnets. Our family routine returned to normal.

In time, the children left home; and my husband and I agreed to divorce. It really had nothing to do with ours being a blended family as much as it was about our personal differences. No amount of effort seemed to overcome them, and we went our separate ways. But when I look back on that time in my life, one of my sweetest memories is of a chill autumn night when the six of us said goodbye to Patches.

What I Didn't Write

When it comes to writing, call me a procrastinator. I tell myself the moment isn't right, that I am too busy with other things, that I need a flaming sunset for inspiration. I want to believe these things are true, but really they are all excuses. The moment will never get any better, and I can always fill my hours with activities that work against the quiet task of writing.

The truth is that good writing, even modestly acceptable writing, requires sitting down and doing it. Now. Regularly. With commitment. It's like the hour a day at the piano that is the foundation of the recital. Or the one thousand sandlot hits that give a batter his eye. It's the repetitive, over-and-over assembly of stitches into needlework that creates a whole from bits.

What have I put off writing?

There is the essay about returning to the farmhouse of my youth to find it inhabited by strangers. They thought I was the strange one when I asked what had happened to the porch that once spanned the front of the shabby shake shingle two-story structure. The porch had been the ancient house's saving grace. Without it, nothing softened the harsh brown shingles and dirty narrow windows.

The current tenants were renters who were just passing through, waiting for their luck to change, then moving on. They knew nothing of the porch. In the dullness of a gray afternoon, I walked around the outside of the entire building pointing to a window here and telling them that was the living room, pointing to a window there and describing the dining room. Here was the wall where the stairwell, steep and dark, went up to the second floor landing and the first of three bedrooms. The one at the top of the stairs had been my room.

I was six years old when I went to live in that house. At the time, my mother had no place to put me, and the elderly aunt and uncle who owned that farm took me in. Now my mother, my aunt, and my uncle are all dead, and I am the last person in my family to have lived on that farm. If I don't put down what it was like, a little piece of history will meet the same fate as the porch.

Then there is a story that runs around in my head based on the ten years I spent living with stepchildren. I say story, because I want to write about the experience from the older stepdaughter's point of view rather than my own. I've already written unpublished reams on what being a stepmother was like. But how did two little girls feel when the court decided they should come and live with their father and me and visit their mother only at predetermined times?

The summer they arrived, the older girl was ten in human years. She had already mastered the role of mother to her younger sister, and she had been a parent to her own mother whenever that woman became ill. Slender, almost wispy, the child was street smart, yet a dreamer. Wise and innocent. Incredibly old at a young age.

We had difficulty hitting it off, and I suppose it was because neither she nor her biological mother could find room in their hearts for one more parent. Yet this girl reminded me so much of another little girl who went to live in a shake shingle house on a fifty-acre farm. I never told my stepdaughter that we were more alike than it appeared, because it would not have altered our relationship. But I could have written it down for later.

I could sit down now and begin either of these projects. With quiet introspection, I might recall exactly how I felt in the situation and why it was important. Then I might put the effort on paper; because, as long as there are fingers and pens and loose leaf and determination, words will eventually come.

They may not have been sculpted in the white heat of the moment when passion is high and the senses are alert. They may not capture the initial thought, but only its shadow. They may not come from the reality, but only from the remembering of it.

But, with care and concentration, they can be as good.

15

Tattoo

I'm not the oldest woman to get a tattoo at the Jade Dragon. I'm not even close. So when George, the tattoo artist, tells me he once put a little red ladybug on the wrist of a seventy-year-old woman I figure that, if she could stand the discomfort, at fifty years old I can too.

By then, George and I have come to terms. I have paid my money, a real incentive not to change my mind, and am stretched out in a contraption that resembles a dentist's chair. Jeans hang off my hipbones and my underwear is folded down as far as it can go and not reveal anything.

"How much does it hurt?" I ask.

"Ever had a kid?"

"Yes."

"I think it's less painful, I wouldn't know for sure."

What George knows about childbirth is hearsay; what I know is fact based on empirical evidence. It hurts. A lot. The first time I gave birth my belly stood at the top of a great dip and raced to the bottom every couple minutes for a thirty-six hour roller coaster ride. The second time I gave birth, I blacked out completely. There was no third time.

What George means to say is that this is going to get rough.

I concentrate on staring at the ceiling, try to simulate deep breathing, and remember the classes in yoga and transcendental meditation that are on my life's resume. George readies himself to sculpt around my stretch marks.

How did I get here?

*   *   *   *   *

The idea of a tattoo had been itching around in my brain for ages. I'd scratch a little and it would go away. But the itch always returned. So on a whim I began researching tattoo parlors. I read about this one in a magazine that rated several places for cleanliness, professionalism, quantity of tattoos, and cost. Jade Dragon received high marks in all areas.

When I called for information, I was greeted by a taped male voice, an electronic disclaimer, telling me that Jade Dragon did not tattoo anyone who was under the age of eighteen, was inebriated, or both. Electronic Voice listed the hours the establishment was open, said no appointment was necessary, and launched into a lengthy explanation on how the tattoo artists wore rubber gloves and used only disposable needles for obvious health reasons.

The itch for a tattoo returned around my birthday. It gnawed and bothered until my mind gave in and said, "What better way is there to celebrate surviving half a century? Go for it."

I got in my Volkswagen and stick-shifted to the Jade Dragon. It was a storefront affair on West Belmont with the streetside windows painted over in dense multi-colored designs that prevented passersby from looking in. The parking spot directly in front of the place was empty. I took it as a sign to pursue this crazy idea seriously and squeezed my little car inconspicuously between two larger, sleeker neighbors.

When I first opened the front door to the Jade Dragon, customers and tattoo artists alike reacted as if bright light were a form of shock treatment. Eyes blinked like bats and heads twitched as dark faces, dark clothes, and dark walls absorbed the sunlight that clung to my white T-shirt and cream-colored jeans. My own eyes dialed up, getting used to black on black. The room came into focus.

Thousands of samples of tattoo art hung in racks around the front waiting room and the room to the east of it, each with a number in the lower right hand

17

corner. Several racks had enough different tattoo interpretations of butterflies to rival the actual number in the species. Others confirmed that love as a four-letter word had tremendous graphic potential. Almost every design imaginable was included in this array. I had come with my own idea, the main theme of which had rambled around in my head longer than the urge for a tattoo.

I closed the Jade Dragon's front door and approached a tall counter that bisected the waiting room in two. Bikers and leather aficionados on my side of the divider stared at the racks of tattoos. Some of them, mostly males, stood with one boot pressed to the floor in front of the other, their toughness on public display. A cluster of teenage girls with a coat of suburban polish giggled in the corner. Now that the light from outside had dissipated, no one tossed a second sneer in my direction.

I peered over the counter at a burly man in a black T-shirt whose sleeves were rolled to the shoulders and whose arms displayed equally black tattoos covering them like hair covers most men. He waited for me to speak.

"Can you do original artwork?"

"Is the Pope Catholic?"

The Lord shows up in strange places.

"What do you have in mind?"

"If you have a pencil and paper, I'll show you."

Tattooed arms disappeared under the counter top and reappeared with the requested supplies. Quickly, I scribbled the word 'Someone' in the middle of the paper, all capital letters. Then I framed two sides of it with the square root sign, which some people confuse with the division sign by forgetting the little hook on the end. Above the horizontal line, I wrote the word 'Me,' before turning the paper around for the man to examine. Then I put my own unadorned arms down at my side.

I had drawn this little phrase many times, mostly for friends who didn't quite understand its meaning when asked to explain what they saw. My expectations of this burly gentleman were that he too would puzzle over it, maybe wanting an explanation, maybe not. He didn't have to understand it to duplicate it on my body.

"The square root of someone is me," he said and smiled. "That's cool." My expectations did an acute adjustment. It was clear that people with tattooed arms possess superior intelligence.

"The name's George. I can do that," he said.

"Will it hurt?"

There was no answer as he took the paper and pencil and drew his version, which was similar to mine except that all his letters were the same height. Then he pushed the paper in front of me for approval. Back and forth we went, making one letter straighter here, another rounder there. We talked about color and then added a butterfly as the ultimate symbol of the essence of square root. Finally, we were both happy.

"Where you putting this?" George asked, once he had created a transfer from the design. I stepped back from the counter so he could see more of my five-foot frame and pointed.

"Right here," and my right hand covered the spot on my right front hip.

"Okay," he said. "It costs more there. Let's settle finances first."

George took the pencil we'd been using and did some figuring on scrap paper. He pulled the corners of his mouth this way and that, making his mustache sway back and forth. He seemed to be having trouble naming a price, so he crossed to the back of the room to consult with another, larger version of himself. This second man looked at the artwork with question marks in his eyes. Then he looked at George. The two whispered back and forth briefly before George returned to the counter.

"One hundred twenty-five."

I reached into my wallet and pulled seven new, folded twenty-dollar bills from it. I spread them apart for George to see and laid them on the counter. George took the bills and made them disappear into a cash register, exchanging them for a ten and a five that had definitely landed in a lot of other hands before being placed in mine. It felt as binding as a legal document.

"Uh, George, is there somewhere we can do this in private?"

Lowering my jeans and underwear for a tattoo artist was never a concern, just as it has never been a problem to undress in front of my doctor. But the undecided bikers and giggly teenage gawkers were another factor. If it hurt, I didn't want them to observe my reaction to pain.

Without speaking, George opened a little door in the counter. I stepped over the threshold and followed him to the back of the main room, down a narrow hall, and to the left. Curving left once and then twice, we came to a tiny room with a window onto the front part of the shop. The bikers and gigglers were still visible. But with a sweeping movement of his arms, George grabbed the heavy curtains on either side of the window and pulled them to the middle.

"Undo your jeans and push them down. Roll your underwear down too."

*　　*　　*　　*　　*

He dons rubber gloves, takes the paper transfer of my design, and places it over my right hipbone, avoiding eye contact with the skill of a gynecologist. He hands me a small mirror to study the positioning of the transfer.

"Looks good," I smile from a horizontal position.

With the palm of his hand he pats the transfer firmly in place so that the ink on the down side adheres to my skin when he peels the paper off. Next, he takes a tool that looks like a dentist's drill; but instead of asking me to open wide he says: "You gotta stay perfectly still no matter what."

I try to remember my mantra.

I try to recall the out-of-body experience nitrous oxide always provides as the only benefit of having a cavity filled.

I remind myself I want to do this.

I wanted to do childbirth too.

He sits on a low stool, which puts him face to face with my right hip. I shut my eyes tightly, but can feel him through my eyelids. He leans toward my outstretched leg. With one hand he pulls my skin taut while the other holds the drill and moves in for the actual tattooing. Drill and skin make sharp contact.

I remember tooling leather in college for an art project. The animal that donated skin for my A was separated from it prior to class, but I still feel a sense of kinship. All cows or sheep who ever suffered a brander's iron are my sisters. The millennium that is 20 seconds passes before I squirm, half expecting two of my legs and one arm to be roped together in response.

My eyes can't stand it; they open to look at this assailant. I want to scream, but don't want the tough types in the outer room to hear. I swallow instead. Under his black brows and mustache, George's eyes and mouth arch decidedly downward. Aggravation breaks out on his forehead. His arms rise off my hipbone and his eyes glare into mine.

"I can't get this straight if you wiggle."

I am willing to forgive him this professional flaw.

"You gotta not squirm like that."

"How much longer?"

"The straight lines are the hardest, but I'm almost through with the square root sign. Five more minutes, if you're still."

21

I don't want to be the first person to walk out in the middle of a tattoo. When I'm in that automobile accident that I always change my underwear and socks for and am rushed to the emergency room where my clothes are cut off for a full body examination, I want my tattoo to be all there across my hipbone. I'm betting the trained nurses and doctors in that emergency department will have seen enough clean socks; and the sight of my tattoo will inspire them to work doubly hard to bring me back from life's edge. Come on, I tell myself, five additional minutes isn't that long.

I stare at the sign on the wall above George's head: "Pain is fear leaving the body." I recall the tattoos that spread across George's arms. This man is fearless. He eats nails for breakfast. Pain is his best friend.

He lowers his arms against my torso and legs once more. I grit my teeth and hold my breath for the upcoming eternity. Five seconds, fifteen seconds, thirty. George stops and reaches for a tissue with which to wipe the area. I expel the pent-up air in this nanosecond of relief.

George is ready for more.

It is the longest five minutes in my life. But finally, George puts his tools on the table next to us and heaves a finishing sigh. Pulling off the rubber glovers, he stands and stares admiringly at my hipbone. The pleasure in his eyes is not a lascivious gesture; it is a sign of satisfaction. Then I see a slight hesitation, as if there is something he missed and is considering whether to tackle me again. But the urge passes. He puts his stamp on his work with a final nod of his head and passes me the little mirror.

My hand moves it into place for the viewing. It feels weird to own a tattoo, but it is a good weird. The words and the square root sign are black. The butterfly is multicolored. George has also created a wake of colored swirls that look as if the butterfly is really in motion. They make the black words seem less stark. The skin itself looks tender and red, but George assures me that this goes away in a couple weeks.

I am pleased.

"You'll have to keep this bandaged for the rest of the day," he instructs. "Don't let it rub against your clothing."

With the aplomb of a surgeon, he covers the tattoo with gauze that he Scotch tapes in place. I slip off the chair, carefully roll up my underwear and pull my jeans into place. George hands me a sheet of instructions and a tube of cream that must be applied to the tattoo regularly until the area is no longer tender. The fear that was mine minutes ago has metamorphosed into pride. Already, my mind is forming the answer to the question my friends will ask.

"No, it wasn't bad at all."

I thank George profusely for his skill and patience. We are the only two people in the world who know what is etched under my jeans. In my book, that makes us conspirators. He displays no more emotion than if he'd just measured me for shoes. I take one last look around the little room and extend my hand to George. He takes it briefly as I bless our handshake with a final "Thank you." Thank you because all fear has left my body and pain is now my friend too.

Goodbye, Gary

I was on a roll. My brain and fingers worked feverishly together at the computer, as ideas flowed from one to the other. I was aware of how good it felt to be at work when the jangle of the telephone interrupted my concentration. It took the full four rings to decide whether to let the caller go to voicemail; but at the last second I picked up.

"Hello."

"Anne, it's Gary."

I heard a quick intake of breath.

"I'm calling to say goodbye."

Gary was a business acquaintance. We were not particularly close, but he had come through for me a couple years back when I was in a real jam.

"Are you moving?"

"No, I'm dying."

I smiled, and it was probably good that he couldn't see through the telephone line. But I was struck with how typical this was. Gary had the ability to cut through the muck and the mess and assess a situation clearly. If he said he was dying, then it was so.

I didn't say anything, but he didn't seem to mind.

"The cancer has spread," he finally said.

"I'm so sorry," I told him. And I truly was.

I thought of how I'd turned to him in need. My client had given me part of my fee which I, in turn, gave to a graphic designer whom I'd subcontracted to help me. How was I to know the designer would take my money and never deliver the work? Frantic, I went to see Gary at his office. Inside half an hour and several cigarettes, Gary arranged for another designer to do the work for free, provided I did some writing for free in exchange. I would always be grateful.

The last time I saw Gary was about a year ago. I'd asked him to lunch, mostly to catch up on each other's lives; and we agreed to meet at some nondescript coffee shop near his office. I don't remember the name; but I do remember that, when I arrived, Gary was already sitting in a booth in the nonsmoking section. The other strange thing was that his head was completely bald.

Over lunch I thanked him again for saving me. It was then that he talked about discovering he had lung cancer. There had been surgery; and, after that, he'd managed to give up his two-pack-a-day habit. Everything was under control, he told me. The additional treatments were almost complete; he was in remission; and, just in case, his wife Susan was coming into the business.

We hadn't talk since. Until this phone call.

"Is there anything I can do?" I asked. It felt like a lame thing to say, but no other words came to mind.

"I have a favor to ask," Gary said. He paused for a split second, then said: "If Susan needs help, can I count on you?"

"Gary, you know I'll be there. Just have her call."

"No, Anne. She doesn't know you. She won't call. You must call her. "

I realized I was trying to put the responsibility for doing Gary a favor onto him or his wife; maybe I was even trying to avoid it altogether. But he saw through it.

"You must call her," he repeated.

"I promise," I said. "Writer's word."

"Thanks. I don't have a lot of time left. I'm telling my friends that I'm not going to make it, because I want them to hear it from me personally and not from some third party or after the fact. Then I'm going to spend the remaining time with Susan and my daughters."

Never before had anybody telephoned me with a message like that.

"I'm flattered to be included among your friends, " I told him. "And whatever Susan needs from me, I'll be there."

"I wanted to hear it. Thanks, Anne. I've enjoyed being your friend too. I won't call again. This is goodbye."

"Goodbye, Gary."

I put the receiver down and stared at my computer. The work on the screen no longer held my interest. Instead I clicked on the new document icon and began to write an essay about my friend. The opening sentence was: "Gary showed me that life is mostly about looking reality in the eye and not being the first to blink."

Writer's Block

The dog-eared paperback caught my eye. It lay on the shelf at shoulder height, so that I couldn't miss it, as I searched for something else on my jam-packed bookcase. Seeing her book, *Writing Down the Bones,* made me realize I hadn't read Natalie Goldberg in a long time. I wondered what she is writing about these days, or maybe she is taking a break.

I hope not, because I need a good example right now.

My friendship with Natalie is one-sided. I am simply one woman in her larger reading audience who has found a friend, a supporter, for writing. Write every day, she urges. Even if it is only for ten minutes, just to keep the wrists supple and the creative juices flowing. Write everywhere, she encourages. Great words hang out near coffeehouses and park benches and window seats. Use a writing instrument instead of a computer, the better to feel the process.

Write about anything. The dirty collar on the shirt of the man in front of you on the bus. The ending to the dream you were having when the alarm shrilled reveille. The happiest moment of your life. The most miserable.

Mostly, forget about being famous and write as if your life depends on it.

Once I spent a whole year writing like that. Got one of those blank books with lines in it and filled them with ten minute blocks. Every day. At first the blocks consisted of neatly arranged words that resembled a carefully planned flower garden, each letter just so. But soon, more like weeds, they filled the pages. Finally, clinging like kudzu, the words spilled over from one page to the next, choking the lines. According to Natalie Goldberg's instructions, they were uncensored, unedited, unfettered. I even gave my book a title that reflected where I was in life: *Halcyon Days.*

Halcyons are mythical birds that nest on the sea where it is peaceful and calm during the winter solstice. And that's what my life was that particular year. By

27

choice, I was alone. My problems with my second ex were more memory than reality, and no one else had vied seriously to take his place. There were no obligatory television shows to watch together or after-work dinners to share. No commitments either. Only long evenings on my hands.

So I turned inward for company and spent hours reading. I renewed my acquaintance with authors who were old friends and took up with some who were new to me. Even when I didn't fully appreciate their work, I admired their tenacity; for if reading is a solitary experience, how much more so is writing.

I'd always struggled to find both the time and energy for it, especially when I was emotionally involved with someone. The interest was always there, but often it lay fallow for months at a time. Several spiral notebooks are crammed on another shelf to prove it. All of them start with the following entry or some variation on the theme:

"Today is [Fill in the date; it doesn't matter what date] *and I am launching my writing career. I know I've said this before, but this time it's for real. I can do it."*

A couple notebooks are painfully empty beyond the first few sentences. Others have several pages filled with my curly handwriting. But none is more than half filled. What they really proved was that I was miserable at meeting self-imposed writing deadlines and the years were slipping by.

That's when I decided to follow Natalie's advice. Among the several books she's written is *Writing Down the Bones*, which I had given my mother in paperback as a birthday gift. As was her habit, Mother gave the very same book back to me for a Christmas gift a couple years later. What could I do but accept that Natalie's book was really meant for me? I read it in a minimum of sittings and, filled with inspiration, tried once more. The first entry in *Halcyon Days* reads:

May 30   *"Memorial Day with Kevin and Elizabeth.   Golden Nugget. Breakfast. Montrose Harbor. Sun. Jade Dragon. Tattoo. Leona's. Pizza. Home! ... and summer begins."*

This time there were no promises of filling notebooks. It wasn't about *wanting* to be a writer as much as it was simply starting the business of being one.

That was five years ago. I've done a lot of writing since then. I've had several essays published and many more returned. I sent the novel that represents another year of my life to an agent, only to have it rejected. Soundly rejected too, with a whine in the voice that I'd bothered her in the first place. And that's the reason I've used for not sitting down and writing this past month. Besides, the seasons are about to change and I'm not inspired.

Until now, when Natalie's book caught my eye, like a former teacher you run into on the street who silently reminds you of your potential. Who rejects that old excuse called Writer's Block.

Ah, Natalie, you are here when I need you. I don't even have to take the book off the shelf. I know what you will say.

You will tell me to begin again.

Meeting My Father

Two years ago, on the kind of bright August day that burns your eyes, I met my father. It was our first encounter in forty-five years.

He was seventy-eight. I was forty-nine.

For a long while after that, I tried to take the memories of the years he wasn't around and the impressions of that one meeting and create something concrete from them. Like a mental box for holding photographs from the imagination. Or a child's fairytale where the prince finally rescues the princess. I tried writing about this meeting and what it meant at least one hundred times in my head and half that many times on paper. I wanted a neatly wrapped beginning and an end.

Finally I gave up, because no matter how I moved them this way and that, there were only bits and pieces.

*   *   *   *   *

What was it like to grow up without a father? Today's statistics suggest it is commonplace; but in the nineteen fifties and sixties, it was unusual. I was often the only student in class whose father didn't live with her and this seemed difficult for others to understand.

The Catholic high school I attended in Little Rock, Arkansas, held a Father-Daughter Banquet every spring; but, not having an escort, I had never gone. In our senior year, my best friend, Rosemary, asked her father if he would take me to the banquet with them and he agreed. He wondered why they had never thought of this before. But when Rosemary gave her RSVP to the nun in charge, Sister told her I could not go because that man was not my father.

*   *   *   *   *

"You were abandoned," said a therapist years later.

I never felt that way, although my mother said he deserted us shortly after I was born. The only other thing she told me about him was that he loved to dance. I often wondered if that was part of the reason I love to dance. Or why I married the two men I did. Both of them were wonderful dancers in whose outstretched arms I forgave their other transgressions.

Beyond this one piece of information, Mother refused to discuss him, perhaps hoping I wouldn't notice his absence. But the silence that surrounded his name made him even more present to a little girl with long, blonde pigtails.

No, I was never abandoned.

*   *   *   *   *

One day in the middle of nowhere, the telephone jangled and I answered on the third ring. I was sitting in the basement of my suburban home surrounded by the dirty laundry an active family produces.

"Hello."

"Anne?"

"Speaking."

"This is your father."

What do you say to a greeting like that?

I asked for proof.

"Louise," he said.

Louise was a relative on my father's side that I had managed to contact in my early adult years when the urge to find him had been strong and I was out from under my mother's carefully maintained attitude that he didn't exist. But the search, which was only half-hearted in its most intense days, was discarded as I

31

married and had a family of my own. Eventually Louise and I reduced our contact to holiday greetings. Then to nothing.

"She gave me your telephone number before she died and I held onto it," the man claiming to be my father said. "I only hoped you wouldn't move before I got enough courage to call."

I have lived in over twenty places. Disconnected telephone numbers are a way of life, and keeping in contact with me requires active interest on both sides. Who knows what kept me semi-rooted until his courage acquired critical mass?

It was six years from that first telephone call through birthday cards and Christmas greetings and photos back and forth before we decided to meet. Given our ages one could argue that we should have proceeded more quickly, but this pace seemed right. I'm not sure we ever wanted to force ourselves into each other's lives as much as we simply wanted to be in touch.

Gordon and Anne.

*　*　*　*　*

August 23 was a hot, clear day. The kind you sweat through dozens of times in a steamy summer. I had flown to San Francisco to see my younger son and celebrate his birthday. One day while he was at work I rented a car to drive the hour inland to my father's house alone. As the car cruised along, it gave me time to compartmentalize my visit with my son, temporarily put it on a mental shelf, and focus on the coming afternoon.

In my mind, this meeting was to be a free-flow event. I wasn't coming to chastise him for leaving long ago. Nor did I intend to interrogate him about his reasons. There was no more emotional attachment to this visit than to the many I'd made to museums over the years to learn more about art or natural science or history. More than anything, simple curiosity drove the desire.

I will never forget my first impression on the front porch of that two-story house in Dublin, California. As my fingers pressed the doorbell, I heard it chime somewhere inside. There was no sound of feet coming to answer, but within moments he opened the door.

Years ago there was a television program called "This Is Your Life." When the guest of honor was reunited with some long lost relative or special friend, they hugged spontaneously and the audience smiled collectively. But today there was no spontaneous sense of recognition.

We stood tentatively looking at each other across the threshold, not knowing what to do next. In spite of the photos he had sent, I would never have recognized this man on the street. Except for one thing.

He had the palest blue eyes.

I have pale blue eyes.

My mother's eyes were brown.

How do you distill in a moment all the years and miles and hearsay? All the questions and fantasies? The prayers both answered and unanswered? What emotion do you pick from the pile and examine before folding it and moving on to the next. Finally, I chose from the stack.

"How about a hug?"

He hesitated slightly.

"Well, why not."

I put my arms under his and around his back and hugged firmly. He reached around me, not pulling me close but just taking what was available in an offhand way. It felt somewhat obligatory, hugging this man who was a stranger and my father at the same time. But it broke the ice on that hot day, and he invited me in.

*   *   *   *   *

33

The formal tour of his home was punctuated with commentary about his second wife's flair for interior design. More than once, he pointed out some special touch she had incorporated into their living space. The wallpaper here had been a favorite pattern, the draperies there had been custom-made. The house was lovely.

"Hope and I were married for over thirty years, " he said. "And we lived in this house over twenty. When she died, I told myself I would stay here till the cat died too. I could move from this place and make it, but I didn't think the cat would survive. So I stayed. Last spring the cat died."

So he had cleaned out the closets and put the house up for sale over the summer. He hadn't thought it would move quickly, but within two weeks a young couple had come and picked and poked through it. They had returned more than once, each time with different questions, and then they had made their offer.

"We're closing soon," he said. "They're a nice couple, but they probably will want to change things. I'll have to get rid of some of Hope's furniture, because it won't fit in a tiny apartment."

*   *   *   *   *

Soon we were sitting in the sunroom off the kitchen at the back of the house. His body filled the aluminum chair fully, but not to overflowing. For a man, he wasn't particularly tall, definitely less than six feet. He rested clean, short hands on his legs just above the knees. His fingers tapped in quiet nervousness. He wore gray slacks and a gray, blue, and white short-sleeved button-down shirt. A rectangular bulge in the left breast pocket of the shirt told me he smoked.

The skin on his hands and forearms was pale. On the back of his right hand was a large purple mark that might have been a recent bruise or a birthmark. It was one of those out-of-the-ordinary features that a little girl in another time might have asked, "Daddy, what's that?"

His skin about the neck and face was similarly pale, with the wrinkles of almost eight decades etched around his mouth and across his forehead. His eyebrows were full and gray. The top of his head was bald, but a strong fringe of gray covered the sides around the ears.

I wondered if he thought I looked like him. I am slight of build with the same pale skin. My hair, with help, approximates the blonde it was in childhood; and my forehead has wrinkles not unlike his own.

*   *   *   *   *

What did we talk about?

Did I mention my two marriages and divorces? Did I tell him that I have two boys who are his natural grandsons? That I finished college and like to travel and like to write even more? I honestly cannot recall the details.

Mostly it's the feelings that have stuck with me.

He talked with a calm acceptance for things past that hadn't turned out as the people involved might have wished. There was no bitterness in his voice as he remembered how he had met my mother and they had fallen in love and married. By fleshing out their time together, he gave me a picture of what she was like before I was born. Those were the days when she had no need to wrap silence around her for protection.

He offered very little criticism of the way she did things; and when he did, no animosity clung to his words. She had her idiosyncrasies, to be sure, but he accepted the greater responsibility for their break-up.

"Your mother was a fine woman," he said. "We simply were not at all alike. I think we probably should never have married in the first place. Except that you would not have been born."

I have said that same thing in my heart about the father of my sons.

Silence spread in the air between us, outlined by the smoke from his cigarette. He looked at me and suddenly asked:

"You don't know any of this, do you?"

I shook my head.

"I only know that you were a wonderful dancer."

He smiled.

He told me how my mother and he stayed awake all night listening to the invasion of Normandy on the radio the night before I was born. It was D-Day, June 6, 1944. Men were dying far from home on French beaches, and I was coming into the world.

He told me he likes butter on three things: scrambled eggs, mashed potatoes, and popcorn. He told me we never, ever spent a Christmas together.

"Once, when you were about five," he said, "I sent a little bathrobe to you for Christmas. You were living with your grandparents then. I know you got it; because a week or so later, it was returned to me but not in the same packaging."

*   *   *   *   *

Late lunch found us at a Chinese restaurant near his house enjoying a bottle of wine and the Oriental buffet. We had begun to grow accustomed to each other, and our conversation wove back and forth between the past and present like old friends' talk often does. More than once, it switched from my mother to Hope to me and back again.

36

My parents were married in a Catholic Church, something my mother later regretted because without an annulment she would never be able to marry again in the church's good graces. Catholics believe marriage is forever unless you can prove there are certain extenuating circumstances. My mother had tried more than once.

"I never understood her devotion to religion," he said. "Last year, I got a notice in the mail that she was still seeking an annulment of our marriage after all these years. The diocese where she filed the petition sent me pages of questions to fill out. I started filling them out, but it was a hard task.

"Finally I gave up and took the whole packet to the local parish church. I told the priest everything in her file was accurate and that I hoped she got her annulment."

For the record, she had.

He shrugged and we sat in another silence. Then he lit a cigarette and thoughtfully closed the matchbook that was engraved with the restaurant's name and handed it to me. It was the first thing that he actually gave me.

"After a while, I figured your mother wasn't going to make it easy to see you, so I stopped trying. Do you realize we have never spent a Christmas together?"

"Yes, you mentioned that before."

"Hope and I spent many Christmases in our house. Then it was the cat and me. Now I spend them alone. And this year, I won't even be in the house.

"Hope used to make Styrofoam Christmas ornaments by the dozens. Decorated them with sequins. They were beautiful. You would have liked her. Everybody did."

And there was such pride in his voice that I wished he might have known some of my accomplishments well enough to display the same affection.

Between trips to the buffet, I said:

"When you move and are cleaning house, I'd like one of those ornaments Hope made. It isn't the same as having spent time together at the holidays, but it would be a reminder that we finally met. I'll never be in your house again, so having something from it would be special."

*   *   *   *   *

As shadows played tag across the valley, I drove him back to the house. We lingered in the driveway, feeling as awkward about saying goodbye as we had felt about saying hello.

"You'll keep in touch?" he asked, as if the afternoon's revelations might make me reluctant. "I'm not much of a letter writer, but you can call collect anytime. I'll call you too."

His hand was on the door handle, and his body was in position to climb out of the car. But at the last minute, he turned back. With both arms, he reached across to hug me. I hugged back, and this time it was like I imagined a hug between a father and his daughter should feel. He got out of the car without another word, and I waited until he was inside before shifting into reverse. He never looked back, and I was glad because tears trailed slowly and steadily down my cheeks.

Since then, I've never called collect. I prefer to put thoughts on paper to be read and reread, so I write letters as the spirit moves and he calls in return. It works.

*   *   *   *   *

The December after my visit, a small brown package arrived unnoticed in the rush of glittery holiday mail. It was the size of a stationary box, and it had not been treated kindly during its journey to my door. The return address held no clue to its sender, since rain had smudged it beyond recognition. Removing the outer brown paper, I wondered who would risk sending something in such a fragile container.

But once the lid was off, I knew. The ornament lay on a bed of flattened tissues, possibly the same ones it was packed and put away in at the end of other Christmas seasons. It was the shape of a locomotive and the white Styrofoam was decorated with multicolored sequins, each individually applied by my father's wife.

It was the second thing he gave me.

*   *   *   *   *

Sometimes I say the word 'Dad' over and over softly to myself. I suppose if this person has been around from birth, it is easy to use. But I have had to practice. I'm not good speaking it out loud on the phone yet, but I use it in my letters. Last Father's Day, I sent him a card and wrote "Dear Dad" at the top without being surprised one little bit at the phrase.

What will happen next? Who knows? I have no preconceived plan because it works better without expectations. What I do know is this: even if nothing more comes of this relationship, these bits and pieces, small and irregular with no pattern, have provided me with tangible evidence of love and connection and family ties with the man who is my father.

I hope he feels the same about me.

Gracia's Piano

It stood for uncountable years like a sentinel guarding the north living room wall. Upright and silent. I never heard anyone play the piano, though I asked Mother from time to time to show me what she remembered from childhood lessons. She always had the same reply.

"I'm out of practice. But I'm going to take lessons again when I retire. Then I'll play you a little recital."

Finally she retired from the university, but the piano remained silent. If she took lessons, she took them in secret. If she practiced, only the empty house heard.

The piano was almost one hundred years old, crafted from dark wood and carved with scrolls about the front. Its first owner was a young girl named Gracia, who had been trained as a classical pianist while her parents had set lofty sights on a famous career for their daughter. I don't know what happened to the career, but Gracia eventually married. She had one son who wed my mother after both he and she were well past childbearing age and I had long since left home. When Gracia died at age ninety-five, the instrument found its way south to Arkansas and my Mother's house.

Don't ask why I formed an attachment to the piano. I never took a music lesson in my life. But when it joined the weary couch, two dining tables, and eleven chairs arranged like seating for a jury in the living room, that piano became my soulmate. On my semi-annual visits, its presence was as reassuring as if it had been a childhood friend with whom I'd shared special secrets.

I often wished it would tell me what life was like when I wasn't around. Did Mother ever talk about youthful memories of her family gathered around another piano in another era singing Irish songs till the wee hours of the morning? Did she ever play Gracia's piano just for fun? Did she consider spontaneity a special gift?

Mother tended toward compulsiveness. She liked things organized to the point where her Christmas cards were alphabetized by sender's last name. She kept the envelopes too. She also kept to-do lists; and I mean she kept the actual lists. And cottage cheeses containers and rubber bands and empty candy cartons. She had a handwritten record of every telephone call she made in any given month.

Although I left home at twenty-one, Mother's compulsions annoyed me from afar while the clutter that collected in the corners of my life must have surely frustrated her. We solved the tension by avoiding discussions about real issues and decreasing our time together in the name of work and graduate school and pressing engagements. Our routine settled in to one or two weekly telephone conversations and one or two annual visits to the other's home. Spontaneity was not part of the pattern.

We never lived near each other again, so Mother often divulged important information over telephone wires rather than in person. That's why when she started a weekly conversation with, "There is something I want to tell you," nothing seemed out of the ordinary. Ten minutes later, everything had changed. Recent visits to her doctor and even more recent diagnostic tests confirmed inoperable cancer. She had months to live.

There was no single moment when the knowledge of what I should do came to me; it simply evolved. I started visiting her weekly, flying the 700 miles that carefully separated our lives each Friday evening and returning to my own life on Sunday night to face the work week. January froze into February and then melted into March. During those weekends, we sat hour after hour on the living room couch.

Sometimes we'd talk, but real conversation is like playing the piano. It's difficult if you haven't practiced. Even when we attempted it, I usually felt as if I were babbling and she analyzing the sounds for their nonsense value. As her energy ebbed, Mother responded less and dozed more on her half of the couch. I stared more intently at the piano from mine.

We were in our usual private reveries one dusky evening, when Mother whispered.

"I want a Mass said for me. That's all."

She pursed her lips together like she did when I was little and there was nothing more to be said on a particular matter. Her eyes remained closed and her left hand rested on her mouth. She turned her head inward toward the back of the couch and pursed her lips again.

Six weeks later she died in her sleep.

The task of dismantling a parent's life is a lonely one for an only child. After the funeral and memorial service, the days found me meeting with Mother's executor and examining the details of her estate. There were the checking accounts and the new car and the insurance policy. There were the two properties and the retirement fund and the coins I found hidden under the bathroom sink. The stock portfolio and the jewelry and the antiques.

Evenings found me alone and reclining on the couch, staring at the piano.

"I have an idea," I began in the executor's office one afternoon. "About the piano."

By then, we had both realized we were bound to each other solely because of our common tie with Mother. Our first meeting was engineered by her in the days before her illness. She had taken me to his office with the express purpose of introducing her daughter and her accountant and executor to each other in case some need arose in the future. I don't believe she had any inkling of the timeliness of this gathering. She directed us like a policeman in traffic, moving us forward here, holding us up there. We crossed the mental streets she chose; and neither the executor nor I saw a reason to do it differently.

"I don't play the piano and it would cost a fortune to ship it to Chicago," I said. "I want to find a local student who could really benefit from receiving a piano as a gift."

"Don't you want to get it appraised first?" the executor said.

"No."

"You might want to think on this a while. Just in case."

"I have thought on it since the day Mother told me she had cancer. I absolutely do not want the piano appraised, because I do not want to know its monetary worth. Instead, I want to find a student who has a special gift of music that will be lost because of lack of money. I want to give that student the piano, no strings attached. It's worth more to me that way."

Mother had been a college professor. She would have wanted progress evaluations and report cards and thank you notes from the lucky recipient. But when teachers receive their classroom lists each September, they cannot foretell what impact they will have on the students charged to their care. They may think they will help the child in the front seat and never know that the child in the back took away something immutable.

"It's an antique," the executor made one more pass at determining the piano's monetary value. "Might be worth something."

"No. Will you help me find the student?"

His eyes looked over my head to the office wall behind me, as if names of potential recipients would appear there.

"I'll see what I can do."

Two months passed before the subject came up again. In the meantime we found someone to appraise Mother's coin collection and another someone to exterminate the house and a third someone to handle an estate sale. Her clothes were bundled and shipped to a second-hand shop; her jewelry was bequeathed to family members. The executor plodded through legal papers, while I searched for a semblance of the life I'd had before Mother became ill. The piano stood guard.

One Saturday as I worked in the house the executor telephoned.

"I think I've found a good prospect," he said.

My heart smiled. Sifting through Mother's accumulation of things item by item was taking a toll, and this promised a break from the tedium and sadness that engulfed me whenever I returned to her home.

"I tried the college, but no one over there knew of a student who needed a piano. So I tried the high school."

He rambled on.

"Well, don't you know, about a week ago Tim Considine, the band director, called and said he might have found our student. I was hopeful that it might be someone in his program.

"But it wasn't. Tim told me he'd talked with Frances Langston. She's the elementary school music teacher over at Jones. That's a grade school on the south end of town. Mostly poor families live around there. Tim told Frances about your piano.

"I don't know how they came to be discussing it in the first place, but Frances has a student at Jones who plays by ear. Nine years old and never had a music lesson in his life. Family is poor and can't afford such extras. I talked with Frances myself, and from what she said I think the lad meets your criteria. You should talk with her."

It took another twenty minutes, but I wrangled Frances' telephone number from the executor.

"I want to tell you about Frank," Frances said, once I got past her answering machine.

"I want to hear about him."

"About four months ago, Frank came into my classroom during morning break. I teach music at Jones Elementary School. It's considered enrichment. Most of my students just tolerate it, but Frank always seemed to enjoy it.

"This particular morning, he came in my room and asked if he could play the piano during recess. I said yes, thinking he meant just for the day. Well, he started coming in each recess and fiddling with the piano. From the beginning, I was taken with how he approached the instrument, how he seemed to know what keys to play. Finally, I asked if he had ever taken music lessons, and he said 'No,' but his daddy was a preacher and there was a piano at church. Sometimes he was allowed to play that.

"The music that Frank created on my piano was real music. He kept at it too, giving up recess for about a month before I stopped him one morning.

"'Frank, how did you learn to play like that?' I asked him.

"'I listen to music on the radio and pick it out,' he said.

"So I played a small part of a classical piece for him and asked him to duplicate it. He did it perfectly. Then I told him to take the same piece and change it, to improvise. Well, he did exactly that. Without pretension or arrogance. He was in his element. Needless to say, after that I let him come into my classroom whenever it was empty until it got so he was spending every morning and afternoon recess there.

"I wondered how to help him. His family is poor; the parents couldn't afford piano lessons, so I didn't want to set his sights too high. But I also didn't want his talent to go to waste. Finally, I contacted the head of the music department at the university and asked him to test Frank. Had to do a real 'sell' job too. But I wanted someone else to confirm that his talent was real and I wasn't getting carried away."

You could hear it in her voice. Finding a student like this is every music teacher's dream. She filled in the details of the afternoon at the university and how the boy had surprised the head of the music department with his innate ability.

"Sam Driggers, he's head of the music department, said Frank had the potential to be a fine musician; that is, providing he is willing to discipline himself to study the instrument and not just rely on his talent for playing by ear."

"And do you think he is disciplined enough, Frances?"

The pause was the space of a quarter note.

"I think so."

Frances and I went back and forth. She called me with additional information about Frank and his family. I called her for additional telephone numbers. I checked with the head of the university music department myself and confirmed what Frances told me. Called Frank's fourth grade teacher and the principal of the school and the executor. At last, there were no more calls left to make. What was left was the actual gift of the piano.

That Saturday was humid, but Arkansans are used to feeling like soaked washrags in summertime. Mother's street was quiet like always. Her house was silent too. I sat on my end of the couch and stared at the piano, forming words of good bye in my head. Once shaped, they moved automatically from brain to lips.

"Piano, we are almost done. You are moving to a new home. The family that is taking you will be here soon. They have children who love music. Your keys will be cleaned and your insides tuned, and there will be noise and laughter."

I am partial to noise and laughter.

I looked at the piano, as I had done so often before, photographing every detail in the camera of my mind. The Seth Thomas clock chimed four times.

The doorbell rang once. I rose to open the front door for Francis Langston and the Stewart family.

Frances was not the plump, graying, close-to-retirement music teacher that I'd pictured during our telephone conversations. Instead she was young, pretty, dressed in shorts, beaming. On the front porch to her right stood her prodigy in his Sunday best and looking for all the world like the poised student Frances claimed he was. He seemed tall and thin for nine, a brown belt cinching him in half.

Behind him was another woman who could only be his mother. She was dressed in a special occasion blue print sundress, and she held her elbows straight with her hands clasped in front. She beamed too. Several paces behind this little group stood two equally scrubbed young men who had definitely lifted more than one heavy thing in their lives. A shiny red pick-up truck waited in the driveway and two cars sat at the curb in front of the house.

Frances made introductions in the afternoon heat, and then I led everyone into the living room to view the piano. The whir of air conditioning accompanied us. We lined up in a semi-circle each waiting for someone else to say something. At last, Frances did the honors.

"Frank, what about playing that piece you played for me in school. It's been a while, but I bet you remember it, don't you? You could see how the piano sounds."

He looked at her and it was clear that even if he did not want to play in front of a strange woman in a home he'd never visited before, he would do it. He would do absolutely anything for her. He stepped forward from our half circle and sat down on the piano stool. It was too low, so Frances and I scrambled to find something for him to sit on. The tension eased and then dissipated as the audience laughed. We situated Frank on top of a dozen magazines and stepped back into our places.

47

This was Frank's cue. He raised his slender brown hands over the keys like an experienced pianist, then lowered them and began to play. With confidence, but not bravado. With innocence, but not immaturity. I shut my eyes and concentrated while Frank played his own composition based on Bach. It wasn't perfect, even I could tell that. But it was clearly more than a child banging away. There was potential. He played perhaps five minutes, repeating the composition twice and then concluding it. Applause burst from our admiring group, and he stood to take a little bow.

Before long, the two men who had come with Frank and his mother were pushing the piano across the living room carpet toward the front door. It had taken a moment to gain momentum, since the piano's wheels were literally imbedded in the carpet and resisted moving at first. One wheel split in two in protest. But slowly and unevenly, we rolled the piano through the front door, over the sidewalk, and onto the driveway.

The case was solid, six hundred pounds of protection for Frank Stewart's future. It was heavy, and it took all of us to balance one end while we hoisted the other onto the back of the pick-up truck. Pushing and lifting, we made the remaining end follow until the piano rested in the truck, as spent from the effort as we were. One of the men closed the tailgate. Our work finished, we chatted back and forth a few moments, saying innocuous things, making the smallest of small talk.

Finally, Mrs. Stewart said: "We can't thank you enough."

How could I explain that I should be thanking them? That I wanted to give away the piano with no strings attached and the Stewart family had come along to accept it? I reached for Frank's mother as she stood next to me and hugged her hard. Pulling back, I saw her cheeks were moist, and it wasn't from the heat. Our eyes met. She smiled, almost embarrassed, then said:

"We need to leave. The truck must be back by 5:30. Thank you again."

"It's my pleasure." I turned to Frank. "Here, give me a hug too."

There was a flurry as they got into one of the cars that had accompanied the pick-up. Suddenly I remembered the stack of sheet music and the metronome sitting on the dining table.

"Wait," I ordered as I ran into the house to grab them and run back out again.

"Here, these are for you too. They belong with the piano."

Frank stretched his small arms through the window of the car and took them from me, offering one last smile for payment. I watched his mother pull away from the curb and drive down the street with the pick-up truck following. First the car and then the truck turned left at the corner of Fernwood Avenue and disappeared. Frances Langston's car did the same.

I was alone.

I walked slowly into the empty house, because the picture of the piano rolling down the street filled my mind and I did not want to disturb it. I stopped at the living room and stared at the barren space on the far wall, the only reminder that a piano had ever resided there.

At last I had heard it played. Maybe Francis would say it was out of tune, but to me it had been the most beautiful music I'd ever heard. A wave of emotion began gathering at the bottoms of my feet and pushing up through my body like some final crescendo. I crossed the room and stood in the very spot the piano had occupied since arriving at my Mother's home. Something urged me to study the view the piano had those many years of family and guests when they sat on the couch. Slowly I focused on the spot where I used to sit, and then on the place where Mother once lay. A picture of her fading away as cancer spread through her body replaced the one of the piano in my mind. What had she thought during those final days? Was she frightened? Was she sad? It didn't matter. She was gone. The piano and she were gone.

Slowly, then gaining force, the crescendo reached its highest point. Pent up tears escaped from my eyes and rushed to freedom. They were salty and sweet at the same time. They were joy and sorrow. One minute I was crying for the piano and the next minute I was crying for her, my Mother, almost wanting her but not quite. Missing her and letting her go with the furniture and the house and everything else.

My Graduation Address

Last year I received my Master's Degree; and, while the commencement speaker was someone of fame and fortune, I cannot recall a single word he said. Which makes me wonder what I would say under similar circumstances.

Here is what I'd want to share:

I am honored to speak on the occasion of our graduation from Lake Forest College. I prefer the word 'graduation' instead of the word 'commencement,' because the ceremony itself marks more than the beginning, or commencing, of the next phase of our lives. It is also about endings. It acknowledges the time we have spent here on this campus pursuing our degrees and learning about life, though not necessarily in that order.

In a way, this ceremony is the ultimate antonym. It is a beginning and an ending. It is comprised of large and small details. It is happy and sad. We will be the Class of '97 for eternity, and these are the final moments that we will spend together.

Graduation is one of those universal experiences that everyone understands. Whether it is from a local grade school or community high school or the most prestigious of universities, when someone tells you he or she is graduating, you know immediately what they're talking about. Congratulations are in order even if you have no more than a passing acquaintance with the graduate.

Graduation is also a deeply personal and individual thing. Every one of us here arrived at this place by a different route. Along the way, we were exposed to different experiences. I took the route of the returning older student and squeezed my studying in between raising children and working a full time job. It took me many years to get here, but I finally did it.

Most of you probably attended for four or five consecutive years, but even so there were many routes. Some of you came from neighboring high schools;

51

others came from neighboring states and neighboring countries. Perhaps some of you didn't really want to go to college at all, or you wanted to go elsewhere; but you came here because your parents wished it. Yet, in the end, you—and not your parents or anyone else—stuck it out.

You graduate today.

Perhaps some of you transferred here from other schools because of tuition problems or academic problems or family problems. You also graduate today.

And quite possibly there are some in the audience who came and absolutely didn't like it, who couldn't wait to get out of school. But you stayed, and you are graduating too.

Which makes me believe none of us needs great exhortations regarding what to do in the future, because we have been doing it already. We stuck it out. We persevered. We did what we needed to do and got through, whether by the skin of our teeth or with flying colors. We are all here, present and accounted for.

So what should we take with us?

Let me ask you to go inside yourself for a minute and think about the route you took to this graduation day. Somewhere along the way there was at least one person you came in contact with—a professor or staff member or student—who made a positive impact on you. Pull up that person's picture in the computer of your mind and tell yourself in words inside your head what that impact was. Work the words until you are very clear what you gained by having come under that person's influence. It is an influence you might otherwise have missed, had you not come to Lake Forest College.

My own mental screen holds a picture of a history professor.

I always had the opinion that he didn't particularly like women. Being something of a feminist, I resented what I perceived as his making me work harder than the men did. Note that I say "perceived." Ultimately what I learned from being in his classes was the value of working a little harder, rather than simply relying on my natural abilities. This professor pulled more out of me, stretched me to the limit, and shared his knowledge in a way that enhanced my own. It wasn't about gender; it was about ability all along. I am clear on this now.

What I want you to do when you are clear on your person's contribution to your development is to remember it all the days of your life. For me this translates into realizing there will be times when working a little harder is not only called for, but also absolutely necessary to reach my goal. For you it might be the realization that some teacher gave you the benefit of the doubt on a grade and it made all the difference. Or a roommate helped you get through a killer of a class. Or a term paper. Or a broken heart. As another well-known teacher once said, "Go therefore and do likewise."

I have always thought that graduation speeches which remind the listeners to thank their parents or significant others demean both the graduates and their supporters. It is obvious we could not have arrived at this place unassisted. If we have matured in the process, we have offered thanks along the way. We have remembered that this was a team effort in more ways than one. Now, the best way to say thank you is to take the raw tools of the accumulated education at our disposal and fashion them into something, so that our parents and families and friends will continue to be proud of their emotional and financial investment in us.

As a guest speaker at your graduation, I would love to be so quotable that my words stirred your soul and earned a permanent place in your memory. I would be honored if you can recall a single word of mine ten years down the road or five years or even this time next year. Failing this, I ask you to remember that every lesson life will ever teach us was originally offered right here.

Old Women Together

Carol Gartland was a slightly chubby girl of eleven when she first made overtures of friendship to me. I was ten and the new kid in sixth grade. March had made the world bone chilling, and everyone else had already picked a best friend.

Maybe it was because Carol herself had come to St. Louis Cathedral School the previous September and remembered how difficult the first day in a new school is. Maybe it was because her parents were divorced, and some invisible antennae of hers whispered that my parents were divorced too. Or perhaps she recognized another only child when she saw one.

No matter. Carol was my entrée into the circle of girls who ruled the class until we graduated from grammar school and went our different ways in high school.

There were eight of us. In the adolescent pecking order, it was Kathi and Mary Nina, Connie and Carol, Carmen and Q.Z. (a nickname we hung on the second Kathy in the group), Carol and me.

Kathi was our leader. She lived around the corner from the school and her mother worked in the cafeteria during lunchtime. Kathi was quick and clever and always ready to have fun.

Mary Nina was more studious, but just as adventuresome. Her younger brother had Down's Syndrome and her younger sister looked up to all of us with unfailing admiration. But most of all, her parents were home on Friday and Saturday nights and willing to host eight chattering girls for a sleepover. I can't count the bowls of popcorn we made at Mary Nina's house while we shared our most secret thoughts before camping out and falling asleep on the living room floor.

I still have a photograph of the eight of us, bound for the swimming pool to celebrate my birthday one glorious seventh of June. My mother had us pose— four kneeling with four behind – on the sidewalk in front of the building where we lived. We are smiling and carefree, as we should have been on our way to the cool water that muggy St. Louis afternoon.

Years passed and I lost contact with most of the Grade School Eight. But Carol and I kept in touch for the big events in our lives. College graduation, marriage, the birth of children, my two divorces. The death of our mothers.

Especially the death of our mothers.

Hers went on dialysis; mine refused chemotherapy. Hers did whatever Carol and Roger suggested; mine took counsel from nobody. In the end, my mother died first. My life ran ragged; but when I finished with arrangements and the wake and the funeral, I went to my computer screen to find an email from Carol.

"When we lose our parents, we lose part of ourselves," it said. And I thought, how true, especially for only children who have no other anchor to their childhood.

I answered back in a fever: "You have known me longer than anyone. You are my history. Let's share memories as we email back and forth."

And so we began writing down the history of our friendship with a detail here, a story there. I charged Carol with the responsibility of printing out and saving our emails, just as she had saved all the letters we'd written each other over the years.

Carol's mother finally decided against further dialysis and came home from a nursing facility to spend her last days with Carol, Roger, and their son Josh. In less than a week the inevitable occurred.

"Dear Carol," I emailed, "I remember your mother from sixth grade. What I liked best about her was that she accepted you unconditionally. It was a gift.

"I also remember how she let us stay up late and make Chef Boyardee pizzas in your kitchen whenever I slept over. And do you recall the time we got into her make-up and decorated ourselves with rouge and lipstick? That wasn't so bad, except that we got lipstick on the wallpaper above your mother's vanity and thought patting it with powder would solve the problem."

"Mom was cremated," Carol wrote back. "We took her ashes and spread some of them in the front yard. The rest we took to the Mississippi River. I clung to a tree on the bank and tried to sprinkle them into the mighty waters. But I fell in with her."

"You were a wonderful daughter," I wrote back.

When life returned to normal, I finished my Master's Degree and invited Carol to graduation. After the ceremony, she pressed a small rectangular package into my hands. Perhaps it is a book, I thought. Or maybe a calendar.

But it was a black and white photograph of Carol and me taken at Pere Marquette State Park that first summer of our friendship. I'm the fair-haired girl on the right, in cut-off pants and a wrinkled shirt. She's the silky-haired one in shorts and a plaid blouse. My arm is around her shoulders, and her hand reaches up to touch mine. We stand side by side grinning at the photographer, because a Sunday picnic is as good as it gets.

The photo was matted and framed and brought tears to my eyes as I relived in an instant all those years Carol and I have known each other. I reached to hug and hold her, because tears alone did not do justice to what I felt.

"Carol, " I say, "you are my best friend, my history. If I had a sister, it would be you."

"Yes, Kim, " she says. She is the only one in the world who still calls me by my grade school nickname.

"Don't you know we crossed the border from childhood friends to lifelong sisters ages ago?" she says.

These days, Carol and I check in with each other more often. The emails still go back and forth. We travel the three hundred miles between our homes regularly. And we take photographs. In a more recent one, I'm on the left. We are both still grinning.

Recently we made a pact that when her husband and my significant other are gone, we will move in with each other. Carol will cook, because she loves to, and I will clean.

And we will be old women together.

Provence

Remember when you were a kid with your first box of crayons? Someone, maybe a parent or a teacher, explained that blue, red, and yellow were the primary colors, the ones on which all other colors are based.

The area in southern France known as Provence is a grown-up's version of that box of crayons. It is a classroom in basic sights and scents, primary colors, and uncomplicated desires. It's a wonderful place to visit when you feel jaded and out-of-sorts or when you want a reminder about the true colors of life.

The basic sights in Provence include landmasses that are tall enough to be classified as mountains without being ostentatious. Saint Victoria is one such mountain. The mountain itself is devoid of trees and shaped like a triangle with one side standing straight up and another lying horizontally on the ground. You can climb the hypotenuse to the top without lessons in mountain survival.

Saint Victoria provided inspiration to the painter Cezanne on more than one occasion. It isn't known if he ever climbed it, but he certainly painted it. Today, there is a small museum-cafe-gallery-gift shop in the shadow of the mountain where one can compare Cezanne's interpretation of Saint Victoria on a postcard to the real thing outside the window. It may sound silly, but you feel as if you hold some of the inspiration for the artist's work in your hand.

Vineyards blanket Provence's landscape with an intensity that is palpable. Dark green and quiet much of the year, the vineyards blossom and come to life in early fall with workers who pick bunches of purple grapes to fill the backs of ancient trucks. The trucks, in turn, wobble down equally ancient roads to the local cooperative winery. You know it's September without ever seeing a calendar by the scent of color in the air.

The Mediterranean Sea licks the southern boundary of Provence and provides natural harbors in such cities as Toulon, Marseilles, or Martigues.

Toulon and Marseilles, in particular, are commercial shipping ports to North Africa. But what strikes you most is the overwhelming number of sailboats and the almost complete absence of motorboats.

Of course, the harbors are deep enough to accommodate sailboats and the weather is favorable most of the year, except when the Mistral blows into town in October. Even then, in Martigues, the sailboats float up and down the inland canals until the Mistral abates.

Then there are the flowers. For every balcony there are at least two cascades of flowers tumbling over the wrought iron. Baskets and pots congregate in doorways and gather on patios. They collect on windowsills, each one filled with a particular fragrance. Violet, red, yellow, orange, green: the image remains long after the actual name of the flower is forgotten.

Vegetables in Provence refuse to be outdone by the flowers. So they line up in rows on carts that vendors push outside their stores, making the already narrow sidewalks even narrower. Olives and zucchini accompany peppers and carrots to present a palette of color.

Women of all ages carry hemp sacks or plastic ones through the streets. They study an eggplant here, a tomato there. They examine the mushrooms and lift the herbs to their noses. Nothing is prepackaged, so the mistress of the household chooses the ingredients one by one for the main meal. And, just as quickly as the vegetable carts appear in the early morning, around noon they disappear like tents in the Bedouin desert.

Every night the sunset provides a strange finale. It begins as a yellow ball; the sort Van Gogh would have grabbed easel and paints to capture. As the sun slowly descends, a pink aura surrounds it and spreads across the sky, making it the color of a young girl's blush. It lingers and then fades lighter and lighter as the night canvas moves into place. Stars begin to emerge in a connect-the-dot pattern.

Slowly this casual, comfortable life claims you. You forget to wind your watch. Instead you tell time by the vendors in the street or the color of the sky. Your head becomes clear and, with little conscious effort, you pinpoint the important things in life. The really important things. Whatever they are.

I came to Provence the year after my Mother died. It had been a long year, and her needs necessitated putting my own life on a shelf. When her estate was finally settled, my soul and my body went in search of respite. Provence in all its color was balm to both.

Bays-Bowl

You know you really understand something when you are able to explain it clearly to someone else. Not just recite the dictionary definition, but discuss the ins and outs, the essence of the subject.

Take baseball.

As a little girl, I went to a couple games and sat in the clouds watching miniature men run around a big square field. When those around me cheered, I did too. As an adult with sons of my own, I attended every Little League game faithfully for two years when my older boy expressed an interest and ability in the sport. His final, painful achievement was to pitch the winning run to the other team in our town's version of the World Series. Then both he and I moved on to other things.

Purists might argue, but from those experiences I knew the highs and lows of baseball as well as the next person. Consequently, I was a natural to explain the game to my two French friends as we dallied over lunch on a sidewalk in the ancient city of Avignon.

For most of the fourteenth century, Avignon—instead of Rome—was home to the Catholic Popes. The political climate in Italy was more tumultuous than usual, and the French kings enjoyed certain prerogatives with the clergy of the time. When the Archbishop of French Bordeaux was elected Pope in 1305, it wasn't surprising that he never left his homeland. He moved instead to Avignon in 1309. His successors remained there till 1403, consolidating the church's wealth and building additions to the palace as befitted their position. But none of these venerable men held greater responsibility than I did as my friends and I relaxed in a sidewalk café centuries later on a bright afternoon.

We were discussing sports in general, and had already agreed that American soccer is called football in Europe and bowling is probably not derived from bocce ball. Then I mentioned baseball.

Bear in mind that all of this conversation was being conducted in French: Bernard and Eliane using their fluent native abilities; me taking a swing—if you'll pardon the baseball analogy—with my ancient, textbook memories of the same sweet language. All of us pretended to catch every word on the fly.

"Bays - bowl," Bernard repeated, with a question mark at the end of bowl. But it wasn't really a question. French people always raise their voices at the end of a word.

I nodded.

"We don't know it," he said. "Nous ne le connaisons pas."

"It's very philosophical," I replied, remembering to make my voice go up at the end.

What I really meant was that baseball is a thinking man's game and not at all like American football, for which we had not yet determined a mutually agreed-to word, but which I personally believe is played and watched in the States only by unintelligent life forms. I had not mastered the French vocabulary to give justice to this opinion, however, so I'd hoped to capture its essence in the phrase, "C'est tres philosophique."

Bernard took his turn at nodding his head.

But Eliane asked "Pourquoi?"

Why?

Ah, the test. If you really know your subject, you can break it down to its simplest components and make it understandable. You might pause a moment here and there to choose the most exact word, but language is no barrier. In the city of Avignon, I sent up a quick prayer. Then I went to bat. Here, in its literal translation, is what I said.

"It is necessary to have time to think because people (I never did remember the word for players, but it was a small detail.) have a lot of choices when a man at the sack that calls itself home knocks on the ball with the wood. If he knocks the ball very up in the air he can run to the next sack. Altogether, there are four sacks that form a box on the ground. But if a man out in the farm catches the ball before it goes"—And here I made a bouncing gesture with my hand on the table—"then the man who knocked on the ball is finished."

I could tell Bernard and Eliane were spellbound.

"This is not where the thinking commences," I continued. "No, if the man in the farm does not catch the ball before it goes"—and again the same bouncing pantomime—"then the first man rests on the second sack. Another man tries to knock very hard the ball with the wood. If he is successful, he must run to the second sack too. And then the thinking starts, because it is forbidden to have two men on the same sack. The first man on the sack must run to the next sack."

It was here that Bernard asked a salient point.

"How many men are on each side?"

"Oh, Bernard, excuse me. There are nine. Nine men take their chances with the wood and the ball. At the same time, the nine on the other side are all out in the farm. They run everywhere to acquire the ball and send it to their other friends at the sacks. If the ball arrives at the sack before the man who knocked it arrives, then the knocking man is finished. If the knocking man touches all four sacks and no ball arrives, he has a point for his team.

"Then they change places. You can see there is a lot of thinking that is required."

Eliane and Bernard nodded in speechless unison.

I was just warming to the subject, but the server brought our check. After studying it, Bernard began some serious rummaging in his backpack. His forehead furrowed and his lips tightened. For a moment, I thought perhaps the cost of the lunch had stunned him. But he pulled out a wad of the new multicolored French currency and smiled at it. I decided it was the obvious implications of baseball as a form of intellectual development that had taken him aback.

The server returned to accept payment, giving us all an extra moment of deliberation. Bernard and Eliane both grasped the sides of their chairs, looked at each other, and slowly began to rise. Not wanting to overload my two friends, I chose to postpone further discussion of the finer points of baseball—such as innings, strikes, and Harry Caray—for another day.

"Thank you, Anne," Eliane murmured as we wandered away.

Like I said, when you know a subject inside and out, the world appreciates your insights.

1925 Holly

There are enough addresses in my background to certify me as a Gypsy. Some, like 4907 West Pine in St. Louis, Missouri, were simple apartments I shared with my Mother.

Others, like 213 South Harvard in Arlington Heights, Illinois, were the single family dwellings of my early marriage; and one, a split-level in Libertyville, Illinois, even had five bedrooms to accommodate my own growing family.

Each place, in turn sheltered me and mine; and I remember something more than the address about almost every one.

But none of the places I have lived ever acquired the title of home. I mean, a real and traditional home, with vivid memories of stability and love. Something to hold on to. Like Tara in *Gone With the Wind*.

That distinction belongs, hands down, to the painted white house at 1925 Holly Street in Denver, Colorado. She—in French, the word for "house" is feminine, and I choose not to disagree—stands on a rise in the middle of an extra large lot like a queen in a velvet green gown. You could pick her out at soon as you turn onto Holly Street from either direction. I loved it there.

The house was built almost 90 years ago, But, for me, its real history was contained between the day my Aunt Alice and my Uncle Dick moved into it and the day they moved out.

Actual dates are unimportant. In the interim, they celebrated thirty-eight Christmases and an equal number of New Year's. They help four offspring spend the requisite time in childhood before encouraging them to head into the adult world on their own. The sound of grandchildren was perhaps the strongest reminder of the passing years.

My Aunt Alice is my Mother's younger sister. There were six years and a million tiny distinctions between them. My mother was strong-willed and determined; my aunt was accommodating and flexible. My mother found her grounding in academic pursuits; she was a professor at more than one university. My aunt found her grounding in her family; what she taught them was less tangible than term papers and degrees, but no less important.

My mother was a single parent in the days when raising a child alone made her a pioneer. It wasn't a role she chose, but she embraced its responsibilities seriously. With school not in session, summers were always problematic. She had to find adequate day care for me, and day care centers were still a generation into the future.

So Momma regularly sent me to Denver to stay with my aunt and her family, while she remained behind and worked.

The house on Holly Street, where I spent those summers, was made of brick and wood, and painted white, with solid front and back doors. It had three stories plus a basement. Inside were the standard living room, dining, kitchen and breakfast nook on the first floor, with four bedrooms plus a sleeping porch on the second, and an attic above. With the exception of the master bedroom that belonged to my aunt and uncle, each of the bedrooms was assigned to me during different summers.

The one I liked best fronted the house on the second floor. It was oddly shaped, with a large center area and little wings on three sides. Radiator heat warmed the house; and, in this room, the radiator stood in the front wing under a window, making a cozy seat with a view of the street.

The décor was authentic. A four-poster bed dressed in an old-fashioned quilt hand-stitched in the bridal wreath pattern dominated the space. A small rocker comforted the dolls that rested on it. The other furniture—a dresser, side table, and small desk—had all known more glamorous lives in New York City, but they had settled in contentedly.

What I liked most about this room was that it belonged to Kathy. She is my first cousin, my aunt's only daughter, almost twelve years younger than I am. When I stayed in her room, I imagined the security she must have felt growing up in the same house all of her early years. By the time I finished twelfth grade, I had already lived in ten places.

Another summer found me in residence on the back sleeping porch. It was enclosed on all three sides with windows, and on the fourth side a glass door led to a neighboring bedroom. The width of the porch just accommodated a single bed, while the length of it held bookcases filled with great reading material, scrapbooks, and other collectibles.

I never looked at a single one. Instead, I spent that summer daydreaming about my first serious college boyfriend a thousand miles away, while staring at the flowers, trees, and laundry lines that were always in full bloom.

My cousins changed bedrooms regularly, and the attic was usually reserved for the one who was about to leave for college. With its own bathroom, it was clearly the pre-flight-from-the-nest experience.

I was an old married woman of twenty-two when I slept in the third-floor attic. My new husband (no, not the boyfriend I'd dreamed of) and I visited that particular fall, and there was no current resident. So we temporarily claimed it for our own and moved the two twin beds together, sleeping across them.

The attic bathroom could have come from an old-fashioned Sears mail order catalog. An extra-long, claw footed tub reminded bathers that the house was built early in the century. An old-fashioned scale, the kind with maneuverable weights, stood opposite the tub. And a half-moon window provided perfect spying on the street below when the bathroom was not otherwise occupied.

I can remember another thousand details about 1925, compiled from the summers of childhood and the more random visits of adulthood. The Gibson Girl that was framed and hung in the half-bath off the kitchen must have watched my aunt repair her lipstick at least once a day. The intercom never worked and the laundry chute, thank goodness, did. Then there was a water heater, which struggled daily with six family members, and a temperamental sprinkling system.

Over the years, each room was redone as carpet lost its sheen and upholstery collected stains. The main floor had a cherry red period, then a lime green period, followed by a more neutral beige period. Hardwood floors were covered and uncovered.

But the feelings never changed. Family photos always returned to the landing. The grandfather clock in the foyer chimed every quarter hour. Books and more books lined the walls. Laughter competed with the grandfather clock for frequency. A sense of the familiar, and of this family, overrode all.

There were formal dinners in the dining room. Classical music in the living room. Preparations for day trips to the mountains. Greater preparations for my cousins' weddings.

A couple years ago, my aunt and uncle—now both in their seventies—sold their three-story house and moved into a condominium a few miles away.

It has a beautiful view; and everything, including the water heater, is adequate and in working order. I think it is wonderful that they made this move together, rather than one of them doing it alone. I'm happy for them.

But I must admit that, even if they stay there another thirty-eight years, I will never, ever feel for their new home as I do for 1925 Holly Street.

Christmas In The Funeral Home

I left Chicago in the early hours of December twenty-fifth for Coldwater, Michigan, and the Putnam Funeral Home. Like a tardy Wise Man, I knew my destination but was uncertain of what awaited me there.

The roads were dry and deserted as my red Saturn skimmed East out of Illinois and onto the Indiana Tollway. They were just a little less deserted when I turned the car North into Michigan three hours later. My stereo filled the inside of my car with Christmas music while snow as soft as silk draped the landscape outside.

Coldwater nestles in south central Michigan, just north of the Indiana line. I'd never been there, but I've spent a lot of time on back roads in the Midwest. Experience told me that Coldwater would fit the profile of a hundred other little towns my journeys have taken me through.

There is always an interstate off to one side, an exit leading to the main street, and a real town square, although it isn't necessarily square. Streets and houses and shops took their time spreading out from the square, which is usually quite old. The interstate is relatively new. The supermarket is apt to be locally owned, although Wal-Mart has staked its claim in some places. Stoplights, where they exist, could break down, and nobody would behave differently. Large leafy trees are valued, as is stability. Sidewalks are not so important.

It was the first Christmas since my mother died. The previous year I had journeyed West to be with her and make sure the holiday was special. This year, I was on my way to share Christmas with my companion, Earl, and his family in a funeral home. We were not gathering to grieve or attend a service. We were coming together to celebrate.

It seemed strange.

I have never known a funeral director personally, although I spent considerable time with one after Mother's death. But that was a professional relationship; and I hadn't, for one iota of a second, considered that the funeral director had a personal life. Did he shop at the local department store or attend parent-teacher conferences or celebrate holidays? I never looked beyond his business demeanor.

But I knew Mark as Earl's son-in-law. He also owns three funeral homes, and makes his own home inside the Coldwater one which he shares with his wife, Adaire, who happens to be Earl's daughter. Earl himself had gone ahead a couple days before to be with them. The plans were that I was to follow.

"You'll know the house right away," Earl said by way of directions. "In most communities, the funeral home is always well maintained. So just look for the nicest place in the center of town." Mark was a little more detailed, providing a map from my home to his, as well as written instructions on where to park and which door led to the family's living quarters.

It was late Christmas morning when I reached Coldwater. I pulled into the Putnam Funeral Home driveway and studied the light-gray stucco colonial. Earl was right; it was well maintained. Solid. Proud. A house Norman Rockwell would love.

When I arrived, the Putnams were already gathered in the living room of their garden apartment, taking turns relieving presents of their outer wrappings. They welcomed me in, relieved me of my own outer wrapping, and cleared a place on the couch. A glass of champagne pressed its way into my hand. A brightly-papered gift claimed my lap.

This was a funeral home, a place associated with death rather than birth. A place we come to at the end of life, not to acknowledge its beginning. But for the next couple hours, we laughed and teased and toasted. We carried on the universal traditions of setting normal routine aside, exchanging gifts, and pausing to simply be together.

After the final gift was dispersed, Mark excused himself and disappeared up a flight of stairs where a door at the top led to his professional world. Three people had died in the past twenty-four hours, and there was work to do.

Mark is a precise, yet intuitive, individual. He wears monogrammed shirts, notices when things don't match, and prefers to live life in first class. He treats his clients the same way. He remembers peoples' names and senses the degree to which they are distraught. His antennae are always up, because he works in a world where distraught is the norm. Burying people is his trade; helping those left behind is his calling.

* * * * *

Mark's father was also a funeral director. He bought and put his name on the house at 11 East Chicago Street in 1946. In those days, the mortuary profession literally obligated a family to reside in the funeral home, so that someone was always available for the ever-impending telephone call. Death's call.

Society regularly reminds us that physicians and policemen and firemen are professionals whose work requires they be on call. But none of these people actually lives at the office or the police station or the firehouse. Yet, no matter the hour or day, when someone passes away, the funeral director is called. The grieving family needs attention immediately. Even if it is the funeral director's son's birthday or his wedding anniversary or Christmas. It is a way of life, as ingrained as if it were inherited on a chromosome.

As children, Mark and his two siblings lived with their parents on the second floor of the Putnam Funeral Home. Depending on what was happening downstairs, there were rules that governed the family's activities. Times when quiet was essential. Times when pets and bicycles and children needed to be invisible. Yet, there were also times when Mom and Dad and the three offspring were like any other family in town. Nobody told me this, but the morning's Christmas celebration confirmed it.

In time, Mark studied mortuary science and then joined his father in the family business. They worked side by side for ten years, burying the prominent and not so prominent from Coldwater and the surrounding areas until Mark buried his own father.

* * * * *

The rest of the day was notable for its normalcy. Family members came and went; some of us dozed while others watched television. Adaire supervised dinner. Mark returned in late afternoon. Although I had never spent Christmas with this family before, the routine was familiar, comforting. If conducting it in a funeral home had any bearing, it was only to heighten the appreciation of sharing good times with loved ones. The three people who lay upstairs no longer had that opportunity. Nor did my Mother. It was the first time I'd thought of her this holiday season, and the memory made me smile.

Evening shadows had condensed as Mark and I sat in one of the main floor viewing parlors, sipping after-dinner coffee. He had finished his additional administrative duties and we both had had our fill of turkey. Earl and Adaire, father and daughter, were off doing other things.

Mark enjoys talking as much as I do, so our conversation curled around and back, from future plans to family history. And around again. From memories to hopes.

"It's my dream to operate the business with my son," Mark said.

How special it is to truly come full circle.

We talked about the house itself, which originally dates to the Civil War, and the many remodelings it has endured. We touched on dying and the question of afterlife. Finally we talked about sleep. Mark rose and flipped the light switch. I followed. Then we said goodnight and headed for our respective rooms.

The funeral home and all its inhabitants were blanketed with peace, and, as I crawled into bed next to Earl, you will never convince me that the angels looking through the bedroom windows were only an illusion.

Deli Delight

The gaudy green and yellow neon sign screamed as loudly as a police siren and had the same result. I pulled my red Volkswagen over to the curb.

MORRIE'S DELI—the sign read—500 ITEMS ON THE MENU!

Beyond the sign, Morrie's (The name has been changed, mostly for self-protection) spread across three storefronts like cream cheese on a bagel.

Five hundred items on the menu, I thought. That doesn't seem so spectacular. I bet the restaurant back home, where I have coffee every morning, could make the same claim if it considered toast with butter and toast with jelly as two separate entries. Scrambled eggs, poached eggs, and over-easy could be three more.

But the sign did catch my attention, I'd grant that to Morrie. Besides, I was a long way from home and my stomach had begun demanding food about thirty miles back. I locked the car and headed toward the restaurant's front door.

Now when I see the name "Morrie" or "Weinstein" or "Silverman" preceding the word "Deli," I assume I'm walking into an honest-to-goodness, old-fashioned Jewish delicatessen. You know the type. The corned beef is piled so high on the rye you have to eat half of it with a fork to fit the sandwich in your mouth. Mayonnaise is served with meat only when Gentiles ask, and the potato pancake is beyond description.

I began to salivate as I pushed "Enter." The door gave way like a gracious host who had been waiting all along just for me. I stepped into a small area, which was dominated by one of those revolving, refrigerated dessert cases, the type that entices you to think about cake or pie for an appetizer. The place was noisy and bustling as waitpersons scrambled around with armfuls of the famous five hundred items.

Yes, this had all the signs of a real deli.

"How many?"

A man with a menu appeared from nowhere. Not wanting to add to the noise level, I raised a forefinger, and he motioned me to follow him. Soon I was seated by the far wall, at a table for two. The man laid the menu on the table in front of one of the chairs and left. I pulled out the other chair and invited my coat to keep me company. Then I sat down.

Morrie's menu was the size of a tabloid newspaper. The outside cover and copious inside pages were all laminated to fend off permanent reminders of previous guests. This made the entire affair stiff and awkward.

I was holding the menu up in front of me when a voice said, "Coffee?"

"Yes, please," I answered without putting the Mother Lode of All Menus down. "Leave room for cream too."

I heard a mug land on the table and coffee go slosh as the waitperson said, "I'll give you a couple minutes. Then I'll be back to take your order."

After adding cream and taking a couple sips, I settled in to study the menu. The outside cover had a headshot of a man whom I imagined to be Morrie. Right where his navel would be were the words MORRIE'S DELI and the address. Under the address was a line drawing of the front of his establishment, and below that was the disclaimer, "If we don't have it, you don't want it."

I turned the page.

Now I am the sort of person who believes in reading the *entire* menu, down to the fine print. I read it very seriously too. It wasn't long before I realized Morrie took his five hundred items equally seriously. In fact, he had numbered every one of them; and, yes, I checked to make sure the numbering system began with one and ended with five hundred. It didn't include beverages, side orders, or desserts either.

But the menu did have some of the oddest combinations of ethnic food I've ever seen. For those who liked Chinese with a little Mexican, there was egg foo yung and salsa. For the Irish who needed a reminder of the Old Country, there was potato soup with matzo balls. Italian cuisine was spiced up with Cajun to create blackened pizza. In a way, this jarred my senses, because I am also the sort of person who dines instead of eats and who is a purist when it comes to mixing cuisines.

Regardless, when the waitperson returned, I was ready.

"I'll have the 339," I told her. "Toasted."

She didn't bat an eye as she refilled my coffee and took the menu away.

A photographic memory must be the most important qualification to work at Morrie's Deli. Or maybe there was a person sitting in a booth near the kitchen who was the intermediary between waitperson and kitchen chef. It was her responsibility to decode the numbers into real food, as waitpersons brought their orders to her.

"The 231 is two eggs, hash browns, bacon, and rye toast," she would say. "The 429 is liver and onions. And the 339 is lox and bagel."

I sipped on my coffee and waited. In time, the waitperson returned with a large plate, which she set down in front of me. My eyes were pleased. My stomach, which had quieted down when it realized I was solving the problem, smiled with anticipation. My hands reached for a knife to spread the cream cheese on the toasted bagel and arrange the lox on top of it.

But what was this? The bagel was barely warm to the touch. The cream cheese was hard; and the lox, although attractively displayed on a lettuce leaf, had ice crystals that split like atoms when I prodded them with my knife.

The marinated olives that accompanied my 339 were chopped instead of whole. They reminded me of a concoction my mother used to make into sandwiches with canned olives and mayonnaise when I went to parochial school in Syracuse, New York a hundred years ago.

I signaled the waitperson who came by my table on her way to the kitchen with an order for a table of eight.

"I asked for the bagel toasted," I said. "Perhaps you should toast the lox too."

She took the plate without saying a word, and I could not tell from her expression if other customers had registered similar complaints. It didn't matter, I silently told myself; you should get what you're paying for.

A few minutes later, the waitperson returned with my plate and a pot of coffee. She laid the first down and filled my mug with the second, then hurried away. I took my fork to the lox. It was devoid of ice crystals but still lay limp and lackluster on the now toasted lettuce. The bagel was warmer but past its prime.

What do you do in a restaurant where eating is popular but dining seems nonexistent? First, you look around to see if you can spot anyone who looks like the photo of the man on the cover of the menu because you want to talk with Morrie. Failing that, you eat what you can and push the balance of the food around the plate to make onlookers think you enjoyed the meal but were not as hungry as you'd originally thought. Then you fold your napkin over the plate, gather your belongings and leave.

I paid at the cashier and headed for my car, berating my stomach for being such a whiner. Listen, I told it, any restaurant which advertises 500 different items on its menu has about 460 too many for its own good. Next time, we will wait until we get home and have peanut butter and jelly. My stomach raised no resistance.

Tug Hill Reunion

Living on Tug Hill in upstate New York requires an act of faith. In winter, snow comes early, like an inconsiderate guest, and stays late. Rain turns roads to pudding. The land has a mind of its own. On the other hand, rolling hills, verdant valleys, and peace in the heart are the earthly rewards for one's beliefs.

Tradition has it that Tug Hill reminded my Irish ancestors of the old country. So my great-great grandparents settled around here before the Civil War. Among the belongings they brought was their Catholic faith, so there has been a church at New Boston on Tug Hill almost as long as McDonalds have inhabited the area.

Time was when both Sts. Peter and Paul Catholic Church and New Boston were thriving communities. In those days, families were large and dependent on each other. My great grandparents, for example, had seventeen children. Thirteen lived to adulthood.

Today New Boston is populated primarily with memories; and the church, although still used, needs tremendous work. Someday, probably sooner than later, the edict will come down to close it. Forever.

It will be a sad day for my family even though few of us are parishioners in the official sense. But every year, we hold a reunion the last Sunday in June. And every year, we begin the day with holy Mass at the church to acknowledge the role it has played in our family's life.

The most recent reunion was this past June when McDonalds converged on Sts. Peter and Paul from as far away as New Mexico, Colorado, and Virginia and as near as Lowville, Watertown, and Copenhagen. We were a Celtic knot of cousins; and, in addition to our annual reunion, we were celebrating the one hundredth anniversary of the dedication of the current church building.

I had come from Chicago and sat in the same pew as my Aunt Alice, just behind my cousin, Monie. My younger cousin, Aaron, sat a few pews in front;

78

Addison and Gert were a few rows in back. I couldn't help but think that the ghosts of all my ancestors, including my Mother and stepfather, were here as well, celebrating the church and ourselves.

Mass began with reassuring familiarity. There was the opening song. The early prayers and responses. The readings from the Bible. And then the homily.

I was sure the Vicar General, who had come to celebrate the Mass, would use the homily to make reference to our family. I was positive he would acknowledge that the church was important to the McDonalds, but also that the McDonalds, and families like ours, were equally important to the church. Without devoted parents passing on their faith to the children in their care, there would be no need for a building like Sts. Peter and Paul. Without gatherings like our reunion, there would be no remembrance of the past or commitment to the future.

But the Vicar General was from Ogdensburg, here at the request of higher authority. He read a letter from his Bishop and then offered thoughts on what the church's walls would say, were they to speak. The walls, he said, would talk about trust in the Lord. About the gift of faith. About the value of religion.

He never once mentioned our family.

The other two priests who were co-officiating the Mass had more local affiliations. One of them was from Copenhagen just down the road, and the other was a member of the McDonald family itself. He was one of two priests our family has produced.

Surely, they will make some comments, I thought, as I heard the Vicar General finish his remarks. But the priest from Copenhagen moved on to the Offertory, while Father Mark McDonald, our own kin, stood in deferential respect to the Vicar General.

They plan to speak after Mass is over, I thought, as we moved into the Introit followed by the Lord's Prayer and the Sign of Peace. But after Communion and the closing hymn, there were no personal words. No acknowledgement. Only the filing out of my relatives, old and young, to shake hands with the Vicar General as he stood in the front doorway.

Now I am not from Tug Hill, except in name. I don't begrudge the official celebration of the church's one hundred years. But I believe that faith is more than buildings and anniversaries and a chance to promote itself. I believe that when your family fills the church and the collection plate, it is proper to notice. I secretly felt disenfranchised.

Next year the McDonald family celebrates 150 years in America. The date is already set. As usual, we'll gather at Sts. Peter and Paul before going to my cousin Dorothy's to share food and good times. We'll recall those who lie in local cemeteries. We'll cling to each other and be grateful. We'll promise to keep in touch.

I only hope that whoever says Mass at New Boston next year acknowledges our family and the act of faith it takes to live on Tug Hill.

High School Friend

Rosemary and I were best friends throughout high school. We spent hours on the telephone in the days when that meant being tethered to a bulky black table model and waiting to share secrets until our parents went to bed. Late at night, we whispered into the phone and poured over the details of our lives, massaging them as only teenage girls can do.

It had been thirteen years since we've seen each other, and that was at the twenty-fifth reunion of our high school graduating class. Which means we left school almost forty years ago and are both firmly entrenched in middle age. The only thing I knew for sure about her now is that she is still married to her original spouse.

So what was my reaction when Rosemary found me via that new communication tool, the Internet, and e-mailed me that she and her husband, Charlie, were coming to Chicago, my hometown, and would I be available for dinner?

Was I happy to hear from Rosemary? Or indifferent? Truthfully, I could have gone either way, which is kind of sad.

Here was a woman who, as a school chum, had meant so much to me. She knew when I kissed a new boyfriend for the first time. She knew when my mother grounded me or when I discovered a new zit. She knew my most private thoughts and I knew hers, even though she had a bevy of sisters in whom she could confide while I had no siblings at all.

What drew us together in that time between childhood and adulthood? I'm not sure I knew then, and I certainly cannot say now. But there is no doubt that we felt a kinship with each other that stood us in good stead at the time, even if the ensuing years have stretched that kinship parchment thin.

In the end, I accepted the dinner invitation.

So Rosemary, her Charlie, my current significant other whose name is Earl, and I met to call a halt to the passage of time between communications. We both brought photos of our children, as if seeing their likenesses at some given point in time made us participants in the growing up process. Since my friend and her husband have a thirty-four year relationship with each other's families, they also brought pictures of siblings and spouses, nieces and nephews, and aging parents. It was wonderful to see because, in another lifetime with an ex-husband, I had known some of these people.

My photo offerings were more meager, not only because Earl and I do not share a lengthy history but also because our family trees are considerably smaller. He is also an only child.

The four of us sat in Su Casa for a couple hours nibbling tourist-quality Mexican fare and laughing at high school memories, catching up on those missing years, and telling each other where our grown children went to college. Then, because all of us had a busy day tomorrow, we opted to retire early, but only after agreeing to get together again before they left town.

I write this in the cocoon of my own home, marveling at the fragility and resilience of friendship. Remembering bits of conversation about this and that.

Both of us returned to school in our middle years and each of us ended up in the communications field. Rosemary was awarded her Ph.D. in communication from the University of Kentucky. I got my Master's from Lake Forest College and have worked in public relations and as a freelance writer much of my adult life.

Through years of experience, we both know how to get someone else to do the talking. We know how to offer empathy and elicit a response. So are we diehard friends or merely curiosities in each other's lives for an evening?

I am still not sure.

I only know those memories of late night high school telephone conversations come flooding back full force. I only know that, although her hair is grayer and her blood pressure higher, Rosemary has the same optimistic viewpoint and soft smile she had at Mount St. Mary's Academy in Little Rock, Arkansas, in the early sixties. I only know it was Rosemary who made the effort to contact me, and I'm glad she did.

Even if I never saw her again—although I think I shall—the value of being with Rosemary for a few short hours lies in remembering that once we shared a time and a place and a sense of intimacy that was real and valuable and special.

Sometimes that is all you should ask of friendship.

My New Confessional

I wait quietly, almost meditatively, in the cramped quarters of the vertical wooden box. My eyes are closed when a sense of vague familiarity comes over me. It prickles the hair on my neck. Makes me sweaty. Then, like an apparition turned real, it becomes clear.

Using a tanning booth is like going to confession.

I haven't confessed my sins recently. But as a young girl attending Catholic grade school followed by Catholic high school followed by Catholic university, I spent more than a passing moment in the mental heat of the confessional, trying to remember my litany of transgressions while waiting for the priest to slide open the little window that separated his part of the larger vertical wooden box from mine. God, I felt vulnerable.

There was always a sense of relief when the few minutes it took to relay my sins and obtain forgiveness were over. I would breathe a sigh, rise from my knees, and escape. Eagerly I sought a pew in the dark afternoon of the church where I sank onto the kneeler to say the prescribed penance and regain composure. There was never empirical evidence, like a scar after surgery, but I had been taught that this ritual repaired my soul. Made it whole again.

Now, the vertical box I frequent is the tanning booth at my health club. Although the main reason is to put a healthy sheen on my body, it has become a substitute ritual for cleansing my soul, and I find it therapeutic on both counts.

Physically, an even tan requires entering the booth with nothing on, except little plastic goggles to protect the eyes. It also means standing for the duration of the session, instead of sitting on the wooden stool that is provided, so that you don't have a "moon" on the backs of your legs.

There isn't a lot of room in the booth, so standing perfectly still is important. I bring a towel to stand on, but its softness on the soles of my feet is the only comfort involved here. The tanning lights on all four sides of the booth are warm. The lights are bright and penetrate the goggles. A motor hums in the background.

There is a certain sense of vulnerability about these conditions, which reminds me of that other vertical box, the one from a former life. Intellectually I understand that there is no little window which opens and reveals a priest's forgiveness in the name of the Lord. There will be no penance either.

Just the same, if someone inadvertently opens the door to the booth, while you are standing there with only protective goggles for clothing, it is awkward, embarrassing, and just as uncomfortable as confessing one's sins. Something you don't really get used to.

Yet, my nakedness reminds me of what is truly important.

I stand for the five to seven minutes I've preselected on a timer and know that no one, absolutely no one, can reach me. I wear no cell phone or beeper. I commune only with myself in a stripped down version. It far outweighs the risk of having another woman open the door on me.

I've begun to use these precious minutes to refocus myself each day. With nothing on or around me, I peel away the worries in my mind. I release the petty concerns and frustrations, and ask myself, "What is important today?"

Sometimes the answer is as simple as smelling a flower or catching a sunset.

Perhaps that's what going to confession was really all about; and maybe the real lesson in all of this is that it's important to find some trigger in your life that provides an opportunity for reflection. Doing is important, but simply standing there and doing nothing is equally important.

Simile Facsimile

Those who lived and wrote in the seventeenth and eighteenth centuries used all the good similes, and the rest of us must struggle to come up with something fresh. It isn't that new words are impossible to coin; in fact, our dictionaries are becoming thicker and thicker with every revised edition. But it is difficult to find a word, a turn of phrase, that is as precise and succinct as the simple similes of yesterday.

I've tried, for instance, to describe a beautiful pool of water. "Clear as crystal" comes to mind. It is simple, yet makes the point. But it is no longer fresh. Yet, what is clearer or more beautiful than real crystal gleaming in the light? Can one get the same pure image with "as clear as the data on the hard drive" or "as clear as the lyrics in a rock song" or "as clear as plastic"?

I truly like the phrase "smart as a whip." It creates an image that blends the quickness of a smart person with the cracking speed of a whip punctuating the air. You know exactly what type of individual you are dealing with. Yet, dare I risk being called hackneyed by using this description?

Ultimately, I must keep trying to make new combinations of words that hold a reader's attention. I must try to describe things in today's vernacular and keep yesterday's phrases from my writing.

But inside me, there is a love for that old simile, that phrase that can't be beat for pure imagery. Think about it the next time you read that something is as cold as ice, as big as a house, as black as night, or as happy as a lark.

Cousin Helen

I hear the clopping of her shoes in the brittle cold before I see her. From the front seat of our new Lexus, I turn to watch Cousin Helen's stick-thin figure maneuver toward us, a black shortie coat wrapped around black pants. I also notice the offending shoes, which are black and made more for summer strolling than winter sidestepping.

This morning, Tennessee is knee-deep in sub-freezing temperatures. It is the talk on the morning radio and the headlines in the Knoxville paper. As I watch Cousin Helen, I don't see any ice on the sidewalk; but nevertheless she slowly, meticulously picks her way to the street.

Finally, she reaches the car where Earl opens the door to the back seat. Before climbing in, she hugs at him; and her pleasure at being together is visible. After words of greeting, Cousin Helen shifts and positions herself inside the car. Earl closes the door. She swipes at invisible dust on her coat and remembers I'm in the front seat. We've only met once, and that was at a family funeral; but she greets me with a generous portion of Southern warmth sprinkled with comments about the weather. An observer would think we'd been friends for years.

"Sure is nice to see you. I'm glad you came with Earl this time," she says, swiping the same invisible dust from my shoulder with a gloved hand. "I can't believe how cold it is. It's just so hard to keep warm."

From where Earl and I come from, snow and cold are seasonal staples. As are the lined boots and heavy coats we're wearing. Once the car is in gear, Earl goes so far as to tell her this, but it is beyond her comprehension. She cannot understand how people possibly live in these temperatures, day after day, all winter long.

Earl and I have driven almost six hundred miles to see his mother, Velma Misch, in Rockwood, Tennessee. It's something he does several times a year.

87

Each time, he picks up Cousin Helen for a visit with Velma. He has tried encouraging her to visit on her own; instead, she talks about shortness of breath and chest pains and not having a ride and not being able to walk that far. When Earl suggests taking a cab, the idea doesn't register.

Earl is her cab.

He will take her to breakfast and then to see his mother, Velma.

We drive the half-mile into downtown Rockwood and park across the street from Junior's Café, the local restaurant that still lets guests sit anywhere and smoke anywhere they wish. From previous visits, I know the food is barely tolerable for Yankee yuppic tastes; but the coffee is fresh and full.

The storefront windows are covered with an awning that keeps sunlight at bay. The entrance is nondescript and simple. Once inside, you can't help but notice the threadbare carpet where waitresses have run back and forth to the kitchen uncountable times. It will be another fifty years before the term "server" is still no longer a foreign concept.

There is no equivalent to hostess, so I walk along one side of the restaurant and claim a booth for us halfway back. Cousin Helen follows and stands by the chosen table trying to decide whether to sit with me or across from me on the other side. You can tell it's a difficult decision. Finally she turns to Earl who has followed her.

"Where you sittin?" she asks.

"Next to you," and she relaxes as the decision is taken out of her hands.

It gives me a chance to look at them, side by side.

They are first cousins. Earl's mother and Helen's father were sister and brother; so it's not surprising that their offspring share the more common features of the family tree. Both are medium height but slight of build, with slender faces and angular limbs. I'd guess Cousin Helen has the same graying hair underneath her bottle black. Both are old enough to draw social security now; but, the harsh

Chicago winters notwithstanding, appearances suggest the years have been kinder to Earl.

We remove coats and scarves, settle in, and study the laminated menus that are dropped at the booth by a passing waitress. I search for something healthy, like grapefruit or oatmeal, although I know bacon and biscuits are the standard fare. Cousin Helen studies the menu as if she's looking for something exotic.

The waitress brings three brown mugs, a full coffeepot, and a pad to take our order.

Earl doesn't waver. He wants the greasiest breakfast money can buy. I give up on health food and order scrambled eggs and a fried pork tenderloin, well done please. Cousin Helen continues to study the menu. Finally, she looks up.

"Do you have Egg Beaters?" she asks.

"No ma'am, we don't have 'em."

Cousin Helen studies the choices again, while the waitress shifts from foot to foot.

"Then I'll have the stuffed corned beef hash."

"We don't have that no more either, though it's on the menu."

There's more shifting from foot to foot and more study of the menu.

"I'll just settle for biscuits and gravy," Cousin Helen says, disappointment flattening her voice, "and water with a lemon."

The waitress removes Helen's mug of coffee and heads for the kitchen. Left to ourselves, it is my job to keep the conversation flowing because I'm the newcomer and can ask questions Earl and Helen already know the answers to.

"Do you come here often?" I assume Cousin Helen comes all the time since this restaurant is only a few blocks from her apartment.

"Huh?"

I repeat the question.

"No, just been here three times, twice with Earl. Once I come with my own family, but it was a long time ago."

"Where do you like to eat," I ask as Earl excuses himself and heads for the men's.

"Huh?"

I wonder if she is hard of hearing or if this is a personal habit, like Earl's quirk of chewing on the inside of his cheeks.

I repeat the question.

"I love Cracker Barrel," Cousin Helen says. "They sure do have good food. Egg Beaters too. The doctor says I shouldn't eat yolks."

As if Cracker Barrel is a magic word, she opens up. Begins to talk and bob her head with descriptions. Tells me not only about the new Cracker Barrel just up the road apiece but also the virtues of her doctor. Says how it replaced the old Cracker Barrel and how everyone loves it. Says she likes her doctor too, especially since he's recommended Egg Beaters.

As if he had timed it, Earl returns just as the food arrives. Fried eggs and slick bacon and triple pancakes and buttered toast are placed in front of him, while two plain biscuits and a cup of gravy are set in front of Cousin Helen. He looks at breakfast with eagerness, she with acceptance. My own order comes next, and conversation ceases altogether.

As young adults Velma and Truman moved north to Chicago from Tennessee. It was during the Great Depression. Work was easier to find in the City of Big Shoulders, and they needed it to survive.

But their hearts stayed behind in the Tennessee hills where life was sweet and close to the bone. Within ten years everyone—except Velma —migrated back home. She fell in love with Ray, a Chicago boy, and stayed behind to marry him in 1932. Earl, their only child, was born in 1935.

In Tennessee, Truman had also married and begun raising a family. He and his wife had four children, but the prettiest child of all was Helen.

Then the war came. Ray was shipped to Germany and Velma went to work. Perhaps she and her son could have left Chicago and gone back to family in Tennessee, but they didn't. Instead the call went out for someone in Tennessee to come to Chicago and care for Earl, who was only seven. Cousin Helen, a high school dropout at fifteen, arrived on the doorstep as the babysitter.

She picks at her biscuit while Earl cleans his plate and signals to the waitress for more coffee. He has an air of command about him. I pass the rest of my tenderloin to his side of the table.

"Don't you drink coffee?" I ask Cousin Helen. By now, I've become accustomed to the requisite "Huh?" before she answers.

"Well, yes, but it has to be decaf and water based. Do you know about water based?"

I shake my head "No," although it seems to me that logically all coffee should be classified as water based.

"I have heart palpitations," she says. "I can't drink regular coffee. A while back, my daughter and I went through the drive-in at McDonald's, and I think I got her coffee instead of mine, because my heart went to jumpin' and a flutterin'. I don't order coffee out no more.

"I did find a place that delivers it to my home. It's water based, you know. But it's seventeen dollars a pound. That's a lot of money. You ever hear of Gevalia?

She shares other stories about the effects of coffee, as if to underscore the seriousness of her heart problems, which became more acute after her husband died unexpectedly. He was mowing the lawn one minute and dying the next. It was too much for Cousin Helen to accept.

"He would be 72," she says wistfully. "I went to Chicago for a week right after he passed."

She puts one hand to her face, covering her mouth mostly, and looks down at her lap as if the strength not to cry will be found there. It's a long minute while Earl looks in her lap too and then places his hand over hers, pulls it from her mouth, squeezes it. The child offering comfort to the babysitter. Oblivious, the waitress jars the moment as she stops by the table and removes our plates. But Cousin Helen has control of herself. Earl gets up to pay the bill.

During the war they went to the Chicago Theatre on weekends, Velma and Helen and Earl. That was long before movies were made for TV. Going to the show meant seeing a live, stage performance as well as something on a big screen. There was the comfort of family during those Saturday afternoons.

Velma's room is at the end of West One at Rockwood Healthcare Center. As the three of us walk the main hall and then turn right onto a secondary one, Cousin Helen's shoes announce our arrival. A doctor turns and looks; two aides stare. Helen moves in along the wall behind Earl and in front of me, as if trying to hide in his shadow. She steps carefully, but her heels still want to flop.

Velma's bed is the one near the door. Earl enters her room first and approaches the small mound of covers that will eventually reveal his mother. We make no effort to be quiet, but she doesn't stir. The rails on the bed are in a permanent up position, so he leans over and says, "Mother, it's Earl. I've brought Cousin Helen to see you."

Slowly from under the mound, there's movement; and two tiny hands push the blankets back. Velma opens her eyes and, after a moment, you can see the light of recognition in them. Yes, this is her son. And her niece.

Helen went home when Earl's dad returned from the war. After Ray worked enough years at the Continental Bank to receive a pension, he and Velma retired to Tennessee. Family connections that had endured thirty years of separation were refitted to the present. Ray and Velma built a house and planted an incredible garden and got together with family, year after year. There was nothing complicated about it.

"Why, darlin', it's nice to see you," she says.

Velma calls everyone "Darlin."

Cousin Helen moves closer as Earl steps back. She flutters like a bird around her aunt and finally settles into the straight-backed chair at the bedside. Her eyes never leave Velma's face, but Velma has already dozed off. Cousin Helen pats the blankets and continues to stare. I stand in the corner, knowing Earl will want to roam the hospital and leave us, the three women, alone.

Ray died a couple years ago. Earl kept his mother in their home as long as it was physically possible.

But gall bladder surgery on the heels of losing her husband blew out what little spark was left in Velma. When she came to Rockwood, she could still walk and feed herself. Now she doesn't leave her bed. Most of the time she sleeps beneath half a dozen blankets and wakens only at mealtime to be fed by an aide. Or to tell whoever will listen that she is cold and needs another cover.

Cousin Helen stares hard. Every so often the intensity of it must pierce Velma's sleep, for she wakes up. Helen takes this as a signal to do something, so she stands and tucks the covers around Velma's shoulders.

"Are you cold?"

Velma nods.

93

"It's so cold out, you just wouldn't believe it," Cousin Helen says. "I had a terrible time stayin' warm last night." She pats Velma's shoulders.

I watch the tenderness between them and marvel. They have little except their memories of the past. They don't expect a lot in the future, just a blanket and the touch of a human hand. But it is enough.

Earl returns from time to time to check on us and then wanders off again to talk with staff members about his mother. He wants to make sure she doesn't hurt or that they know she is a Jehovah's Witness or that they can call him any time of the day or night.

We stay almost an hour with Velma dozing and Helen staring and me watching. I think we make some connection.

When it's time to leave, we kiss Velma goodbye. Cousin Helen wraps her shortie coat tight around her body, as if gathering enough grit to brave the cold.

Can I Sing

It was New York City and I was enrolled in Notre Dame Convent School on West 79th Street. I was small of build with blonde stringy hair. In my somber uniform, I was also perfectionistic in temperament and therefore eager to please. If the teachers said to be quiet in the school's hallways, I actually tiptoed.

The academic side of third grade was easy. So was recess. I had girlfriends to jump rope with and play hopscotch with and catch a ball with in the enclosed courtyard that doubled as a playground at recess.

In religion, I knew all the responses we'd been assigned to memorize from the *Baltimore Catechism* in preparation for our First Holy Communion. I'd even worked ahead with the help of my Grandmother and Grandfather, with whom I lived.

Mine was a view of the world that rewarded effort and did not criticize unnecessarily. Perhaps most adults were kinder to me because I didn't live with either of my parents, but at the time my understanding of reality was that the world was a pretty good place.

Then came music and a nun in black with a starched headpiece. She was ageless and I was seven, one of an entire group of seven-year-olds who filed into her classroom, two by two, each Tuesday and Thursday morning.

Mother Eulodia always started the session with scales, hitting a note on the piano and expecting her charges to duplicate it with their voices. She never explained this; she simply began and expected us to follow. I mimicked the others, since scales were not in our repertoire at home.

It's not that we were without music. My grandparents had an old upright piano in the living room and a radio and even a Victrola that played songs from the musical comedies my family loved. The scores of Rodgers and Hammerstein were like personal friends, as were the Irish Rebellion ballads that every

McDonald knew by heart. But we didn't think of singing from a technical point of view. Rather, we saw it as a time for joyous expression.

Because I was small, I stood in the front row in music class, just to the right of the piano. It was a baby grand. My uniform and face were both scrubbed clean, and I approached music class with the same desire to please as I approached most endeavors.

I can't tell you whether it was the first week of school or the fourteenth or the twenty-fourth. I only remember we had begun to learn little songs for a recital that our families would be invited to attend. We worked hard, trying to blend the words and the notes.

Then it happened.

One regular morning, Mother Eulodia stopped playing the piano and rose from the bench. She looked around as if searching for something truly offensive. As her eyes scanned the room, every third grader present stood with closed mouth, waiting, wondering.

Finally, she moved slowly around the piano and toward the front row. Stopping in front of each child, she seemed to weigh the student's worth. At last, she stopped in front of me.

"Anne," she said, not in an unkind voice, "in the future, pretend you are singing. Only just move your lips and say the words silently."

Then she moved back to the piano and sat down to begin again.

As far as I knew, I had done nothing wrong. Yet I was singled out. Was I such a miserable singer that I didn't get a first warning or second chance? What would my family think at the recital?

I never told them what happened; and, in spite of feeling awkward, I was still eager to please. I went to music twice a week and stood in the front row, but never uttered another sound. From time to time, Mother Eulodia would grace me with a gentle, knowing smile, as if we were in collusion together.

The recital was a success.

* * * * *

It is almost fifty years later, but I can recall how every fiber of my being spent the rest of that music period holding back tears of humiliation. To this day, I am incredibly self-conscious about my voice and never sing where someone else can hear.

My life companion, Earl, says it's a pity, given that I know the words to almost any song and I love to listen to every kind of music. He has tried more than once to encourage me to sing, but his support does not outweigh years of embarrassment.

Finally, this Christmas, Earl gave me a slender envelope with a check inside made out to Velia Botti. Velia is a singing coach. The note that accompanied the check said he had arranged for her to give me one hour of her time. Since I do not believe Earl, at the end of the hour, she will tell me if I can or cannot sing.

Six weeks passed before I mustered enough courage to make the necessary arrangements to come to Velia's studio at two o'clock on Wednesday. She teaches in the Fine Arts Building on South Michigan Avenue. It's a venerable old place where the elevator is still operated by a human instead of by buttons. It reminded me of when I was in college at Loyola University and Mike was on Elevator Number Two.

The operator let me off on the ninth floor, and I heard a piano accompanying a man's voice singing in Italian, beautiful flowing notes that fill the hallway. You didn't have to understand a word to know this person had a gift.

I checked the rooms until I came to #925. Brass numbers were nailed to the door, which was dark wood on the bottom and leaded glass on the top, although time was pulling the glass away from its lead framing. A bench broke the straight lines of the hallway directly across from the door.

The voice that lured me off the elevator was coming from Velia's studio as I sat down to wait. It was ten minutes to two.

What was I doing here? I was wasting Earl's money and this woman's time. If she asked me to sing what would I do? I knew the words to "America" but could not remember the tune. I'd listened to "Ragtime" hundreds of times and my favorite song was "Make Them Hear You," but I could not sing it. Maybe I could do "Twinkle, Twinkle, Little Star."

The door opened and a woman not much taller than I stepped out. She was slender, but not overly so, and wore nondescript jeans with an equally nondescript sweater. Her most striking feature was shoulder-length hair the color of rusted copper. I'd guess she was about my age. She saw me sitting here and crossed the hall reaching her hands forward to touch mine. It would be ungracious not to reach back.

"Ah, Anne," she said, holding my hands in hers. "Just a few more minutes, and I will be with you."

"Take your time." And I've told the instructor what to do.

She returned to the studio, closed the door, and the wondrous voice began singing again. This time, it was a sad, slow piece that enveloped me in its longing.

It also pointed to my inadequacies; somehow I didn't think "Twinkle, Twinkle, Little Star" would do. Nothing would do.

I tried to keep calm by telling myself that sixty minutes from now it would be over, and I never had to come back. Velia could go to her next dinner party telling the tale of the middle-aged woman who came for instruction but who couldn't sing a note. There would be a good laugh when she said, "But she's good at lip-sync-ing."

Just then the piano music and the singer both stopped. I heard Velia giving instruction and the singer, in his normal speaking voice, debating the merit of her advice. After a give-and-take for a minute or so, the door opened and the man who owned the voice stepped over the threshold, Velia following. He paused in front of me and gave her just enough time to introduce us, as if we were equals.

"I really enjoyed your concert." I said. He smiled, said a few words, and headed down the long hall to the elevator.

"Come in, come in," Velia directed with her arm and turned back into her studio. I followed.

Photos covered the walls to my left and right. Most were obviously taken by professional photographers, and many were signed in the corner. These must have been her protegees.

Straight ahead was a wall of windows that looked onto the backs of other buildings. It wasn't a particularly breathtaking sight, but it did let in light and air. A grand piano sat in front of the windows, while a couch occupied the right wall under the photos.

"Let's talk a bit. I want to learn about you," Velia settled comfortably onto the couch at one end while I put down my backpack and coat and positioned myself carefully at the other. I shared the story of my third grade teacher and how I muddled through high school's mandatory chorus praying no one would call on me to sing solo.

"That's always troubled you, made you unhappy," she interrupted. "And now, you want to join a choir, but you have no self-confidence. You need to know if you can do it. That's why you're here."

It wasn't quite that dramatic, but Velia Botti would accept no less of an explanation. To her, life was a drama, and passion was its core.

"I suppose," I told her. "I'd like to know once and for all if I can sing."

What I really wanted to say is that the teacher's ability to teach far outweighed the student's ability to learn.

"And you shall know it," she said, rising from the couch and moving toward the piano. "Come, let's try some scales."

What I wanted her to know is how sorry I was to have bothered her.

She sat on the bench, her fingers resting on the ivory keys. Her hands were manicured and free of jewelry. I stood at the piano's side, stiff and straight, my own hands folded on top of the instrument's casing.

"Can you sing this?" she asked, playing a note in the mid-range. I tried. She played the next note. I tried again, but I could not tell if my sound and the piano's were at all alike. Her face offered no clues either.

We kept at it. From time to time she gave me nonsense syllables to sing.

"Maw, maw, maw, maw, maw."

"Again."

"Maw, maw, maw, maw, maw."

"Again, only this time say, me, me, me, me, me."

It was more work than I thought to listen to the notes she played and try to copy them. I must block out the little voice in my head that said this was all silly. I must concentrate on the sound of the piano. I did it better with my eyes closed and my right forefinger beating the rhythm in space.

Velia continued up the scale and down. Every so often she gave me an instruction.

"Make your mouth like an O."

"Drop your chin."

"Not your head."

Even if she told me I'd never carry a tune, I was experiencing what it's like to try and sing. You must use your entire body, from the toes upward. The legs and torso must be still. The lungs must fill with air. The diaphragm that everyone talks about must push. The ears must listen to the notes. And the vocal chords must make the sounds. I never noticed any of this before.

"Sing out, sing out, try to hit the window."

"Don't be mousy. Sing the way you talk."

She told me to substitute the words "I –I –luh-uv-you" for the nonsense syllables.

"Pretend you're singing to Earl. Tell him how you feel," she said as her right hand waved in the air and her left hand struck the notes.

Half an hour later I was completely exhausted and losing my concentration. She saw it and stopped playing.

"Now you tell me," she said, quietly. "Can you sing?"

The question surprised me. If I knew the answer, I wouldn't have been here.

"If you say I can sing, then I can sing."

She rose and clasped hands. Looked me square in the eye.

"You hit the notes, you followed me. The rest is study and practice. You haven't studied since third grade."

"But can I sing?"

She looked at the ceiling in mock despair.

"I would not have wasted my time. But it comes to this: If you believe you can sing, you can sing."

She made me work for the rest of the hour as if I were one of her serious opera students. Toward the end, I began to know the difference in going up and down the scale. My final challenge was to sing what she had played, only without the piano for accompaniment. It took two times, but I hit it. I believed I heard it too, but the look on her face told me for sure.

I handed over Earl's check. We talked a few minutes and then I retraced my steps to the elevator, down to the lobby, and onto the street. The ghost of my third grade music teacher was exorcised as the sound of "Maw, maw, maw, maw, maw" made its home in my head.

Eating An Elephant

The application was a work of art, filled out front and back, with symmetrical black "X's" carefully touching the corners inside the proper boxes. Earl's signature was uncharacteristically readable.

"What do you think?" he asked as I studied the form, reading each question and its answer. I took my time.

"What do you think?" he repeated.

"I think you should go for it."

"You do, you really do?"

I nodded.

"I've always wanted to be a policeman," he said. "I'd make a good one too."

"You probably would, but there's one thing—"

"I know, I'm sixty-three years old."

It was January 1999 when the City of Chicago announced it would accept applications for the police department. In the past, this announcement had been met with thousands of responses from younger men and women wanting to join the force.

But times changed.

The academic qualifications for eligibility were raised, so some individuals who might have previously considered applying could not. Today's economy is good, and the starting salary of $33,500 isn't as attractive as it once was. And, yes, the Chicago Police Department has had its share of morale and ethics problems.

"I've read all the instructions," Earl said. "You must be at least twenty-three years old, live in the city, and have the equivalent of an Associate's Degree. There is nothing written anywhere about an older age limit."

"Maybe they figure older people self-select themselves out," I said.

"Then why can't I self-select myself in? For the twenty dollar admission fee, I'll take the academic test and go from there."

Earl walked his application form and check to City Hall, not trusting the mails to deliver them on time. Then he purchased several books of sample exams and poured over them as if he were trying to pass the bar or his CPA. When directions for admission to the testing site arrived, he practically memorized them.

"If you're late, you won't be admitted," he read aloud to me. "No beepers, no cell phones, no excuses. Maybe we should do a dry run to the testing facility and see where I can park."

"If you want to," I said. "We can do dinner too."

Half an hour later, we sat in Pegasus, my favorite Greektown restaurant, spreading saganaki on that wonderful bread and reviewing Earl's game plan. Even under normal circumstances, Earl has a lot of nervous energy. He taps his fingers on the tablecloth, rearranges the salt and pepper, and crosses and uncrosses his legs. That night, he was really excited.

"I never dreamed I'd get this chance," he said. "When I was younger, a cop's pay wasn't very good. I had a wife and child to support and needed to make more money. I also learned early in my career that I wasn't the smartest or the fastest, so I decided I would work the hardest and the longest."

This is how Earl finished undergraduate school, one course at a time, in fourteen years. It is how he became a success in the business world. He was always there, chipping away, never giving up, making one more telephone call, checking one more detail, writing one more note.

I could see him applying this principle to his dream.

He calls it eating an elephant.

"Take a task that seems insurmountable or a challenge that seems impossible and pretend it's an elephant," he has told me on more occasions than I care to count. "Don't look at the obstacles. Just concentrate on that elephant. How would you eat it? You'd eat it piece by piece, bite by bite. Slowly."

The first bite was the three-hour multiple-choice test on that Sunday in mid-March of 1999. He came home convinced that he hadn't done well, and consoled himself with the fact that he'd been allowed to take the exam in the first place. It had been at least a passing acquaintance with his dream, if not a full-fledged love affair.

The official letter arrived the end of April.

Earl had passed the academic test with a solid 89 and was eligible for the next phase. It meant filling out more forms, obtaining college transcripts and medical records, and showing up for a physical examination that included drug testing and finger printing.

"Did you know they take a piece of your hair because drugs stay in hair longer than in other parts of the body?" he asked after a day of being poked and prodded. "Did you know they run a check on your prints? Did you know only one person asked how old I was?"

"And what did you say?"

"I'll be sixty-four in August, sir."

"Sir?"

"Yes, everyone is sir."

"And what did Sir say to that?"

"He laughed. Said I could be the first recruit who retires before ever going on the job."

Everyone who passed the basic physical took a power test a couple weeks later. It consisted of four events with minimum standards based on gender and age. For practice purposes, Earl set his goal to qualify with the fifty-to-fifty-nine age group. This meant sitting and extending the arms towards the toes with straight legs, doing 23 sit-ups in a minute, achieving a maximum bench press of seventy percent of his weight, and running a mile and a half in 16.21. Fortunately, Earl had been a serious member of a health club for years.

"I'm hiring a personal trainer to help get me through this," he told me. "Someone who can show me the right way to lift the weights. I'm going to start running regularly at the club too."

"Sounds like a plan," I said. "Are you going to tell anyone you're trying to become a policeman?"

I already knew the answer.

"Let's wait and see. If I make it, I'll have to quit being a real estate broker, because you can't have a second job for the first year. If I don't make it, nobody needs to know, but I'll be in better shape."

And so it went for almost a year. Although Earl often came home uncertain of the outcome, he passed each phase of the admission process. By the time Officer Bradley came to our home for a personal interview, Earl's sixty-fourth birthday had come and gone.

"Why are you doing this?" Officer Bradley asked, as he sat in our living room and stared at the spectacular view from our tenth floor condo. "My supervisor will want to know."

"Life has been good to the Misch family," Earl said. "I want to give something back."

What other soon-to-be-eligible-for-Medicare person gives back by dusting off the dream of his twenties and going after it? What other soon-to-be-sixty-five year old believes a dream is the pilot light under your fire, and you should—as the commercial urges—just do it?

Officer Bradley told Earl that new classes were starting at the Police Academy all the time, and that he could anticipate receiving a letter to join one of them.

"Do you think you ought to tell your family what you're doing?"

It was a question I now asked after each hurdle was cleared.

"Not yet. Not until I get that letter in my hand."

Finally, just as we were going on vacation to San Francisco, the letter of admission to the Academy came. We read it over and over, first skimming paragraph by paragraph, then studying sentence by sentence, finally digesting it word by word. Earl was to start at the Academy on Monday, February 28, 2000.

"Maybe it *is* time to tell the family," he said.

The harbor wore its winter look as we sat in the dining room of the Columbia Yacht Club with Earl's son and daughter, her husband, and his grandson. It's times like these, when gray has become a permanent resident, that it's difficult to remember how exciting the lakefront is in summer.

Earl's announcement caused its own excitement.

"Dad, you've been your own boss for a long time. Do you realize what you're doing? You'll have to take orders," said Son Rich.

"Can we call you 'Officer Grandpa'?" asked Grandson Alex.

"I think it's great," said Daughter Adaire. "You're something else."

But the most telling reaction came from Earl's son-in-law who loves to talk with anyone about anything. When it finally registered that his father-in-law was about to become a police recruit, Mark's mouth dropped open, but not one word squeaked out.

And so began the next phase: actual training.

Generally, a class of recruits stays at the Academy twenty-two weeks learning what it takes to become a police officer. There is the physical training, the weaponry, the study of law, handcuffing technique, practice in simulated situations, and ethics classes. From time to time, there are tests that must be passed before the PPO, probationary police officer, can move to the next level of instruction.

When he came home at the end of the first day, Earl said that graduation would be on June 30. I grabbed a calendar and counted off the weeks.

"But that's only eighteen weeks away," I said.

"If we don't graduate by then, we'll lose some federal funding," he explained. "So they're going to extend each day an extra two hours till further notice."

I shook my head.

Fortunately for Earl, we lived close to the Academy and his commute was easy; but he still rose at 3:45 each morning to study and prepare for the first class at 6 a.m. When he came home between four and five in the afternoon, there was not much energy left. The couch was his only destination. I made dinner and woke him for it.

Afterwards, Earl watched whatever cop program the television offered: NYPD, reruns of NYPD, Homicide: Life on the Street, even the ten o'clock news. Then he'd drag off to bed to begin the routine over again.

Week One became Week Two, which eventually turned into Week Five, and then Week Seven. By Week Nine, Earl and the other recruits were operating on adrenaline. They'd been doing ten hours days at the Academy, five days a week, on top of getting there and getting home. Weekends meant cleaning equipment and studying for tests.

Approximately ten percent of the one hundred twelve members of his class dropped out. Some didn't like it, others had unexpected problems—like a death in the family or a broken leg—that made them eligible to repeat the training at a later date. Those who stuck it out developed a sense of camaraderie. They helped each other survive the rough parts and endure the boring ones.

"Okay, on a scale of one to ten, how was your day?"

It was my new question

"Today, was a five. We ran from the Academy to Sears Tower, dropped on the concrete to do calisthenics, and then ran back to the Academy. I thought I'd die. But I bet the tourists and office workers on their lunch hour enjoyed the show."

The day they made the east Academy lawn into a mud pit and the recruits crawled through it on their backs was also a five.

"We had our sweats on," he said, "By the time we were done, there was mud everywhere, inside and out. Of course, we had to be at our next class in ten minutes, so you should have seen the race for the showers."

He handed me a plastic garbage bag filled with muddy blue clothing.

The Chicago Police Department seems uniform-happy. Besides sweat clothes which are "monogrammed" with his last name across the chest, Earl purchased khaki uniforms for classes at the Academy. Then there were the official blue uniforms for on the job, rain gear, hats, and blues for dress occasions. Add to this the requisite weapon, duty belts, handcuffs, a bulletproof vest, as well as other incidentals; and the bill came to almost four thousand dollars. To be honest, that includes the shirt he bought me which says "Be safe tonight, sleep with a cop."

"I have to holster and unholster my weapon at least two hundred times just to break it in," he answered before I even asked. I had come upon him standing in front of the mirror, feet apart, hands at the ready. Little did I know that we would soon have a paper target above our fireplace for what he called "dry firing." Nor did I know Saturday mornings would be given up to visiting a private range for practice.

"We have to get a score of seventy to pass range," Earl kept holstering and unholstering. "I'm having problems. I just need more time and more practice."

So Earl spent lunch hours at the Academy range until the day he called me mid-morning on a break and said he'd passed.

That day was a ten.

At the April meeting of the Chicago City Council, Mayor Richard M. Daley introduced a proposal that would require all firemen and policemen to retire at age 63. TV and newspaper reports of this proposal noted that it affected approximately sixty to seventy police officers immediately "and one sixty-four year old recruit currently in the Academy."

That night our telephone rang.

"Yes, sir," I heard Earl say. "What do you want me to do?"

It was Mr. Gary Schenkel, Assistant Deputy Superintendent (ADS) of the Academy, who probably doesn't make a habit of calling new recruits at home. But he alerted Earl that a television reporter wanted information about the sixty-four year old recruit. How did he get into the program? How did he feel about the mayor's proposal?

The ADS told Earl he could decide whether to be interviewed or not; it was up to him.

"What about classes," Earl asked. "Am I still in the Academy?"

"As far as we are concerned, you are to report here every morning, business as usual."

We didn't answer the telephone the rest of the night.

The public face on the retirement proposal was that the mayor believes policemen over the age of sixty-three are not capable of the rigorous physical activity associated with their jobs. He hasn't met Earl.

The private face on the proposal is probably a lot more complicated. Wouldn't most policemen that age have been promoted to desk jobs? Are they among the higher paid? What about people who are almost sixty-three but haven't served enough time to be eligible for pensions down the road. Why have mandatory retirement when natural attrition is reducing the police force?

In the middle of May, the Chicago City Council rubber-stamped the mayor's mandatory retirement proposal. Word in the newspapers was that all policemen over sixty-three must retire on December 31, 2000. In the meantime, Earl continued to work toward graduation.

What you've probably realized is that Give Up and Quit are not in Earl's vocabulary. He waited forty years to follow his dream, and now it seemed he would only get to be a policeman for a few months. Re-evaluation wasn't even a consideration, although once in a while he would whisper to me, "If I'd known then what I know now, I'm not sure I would have done this."

You want to know something?

He would have done it anyway.

Today is June 1. He just walked in the door, smiling from head to toe, rather than sighing with exhaustion.

"We had to vote for the recruit we'd most want to be partnered with in the real world," he said. "Everyone wrote their choice on a piece of paper. Then we collected them and tallied the vote. Earl Misch won."

It's the closest I've ever seen him come to absolute elation.

The mayor personally participates in every class's graduation, which is held at Navy Pier; and I can't wait to see his face when he shakes Earl's hand. Then we will party.

We'll take photos and listen to Earl tell cop stories. We'll shake our heads in amazement and pride. Mostly, we'll celebrate that one "senior citizen" saw a chance to realize his long-held dream, even if he has to "retire" with only six months on the job.